2012

Catalyst for Your Spiritual Awakening

About the Author

John J. Liptak is an internationally recognized author and lecturer whose books and assessment instruments have sold millions of copies. Liptak has been interviewed by MSNBC and CNNRadio, and his work has been featured on MSN.com and on the PAX television series, *Success Without a College Degree*. John completed an Ed.D. in Student Personnel Services from Virginia Tech. Visit him online at www.johnliptakjr.com.

2012

CATALYST FOR YOUR SPIRITUAL AWAKENING

USING THE MAYAN TREE OF LIFE TO DISCOVER YOUR HIGHER PURPOSE

JOHN J. LIPTAK, ED.D.

Llewellyn Publications
Woodbury, Minnesota

First Edition
First Printing, 2010

Cover design by Kevin R. Brown
Cover Mayan calendar illustration by Anne Wertheim

Llewellyn is a registered trademark of Llewellyn Worldwide, Ltd.

Library of Congress Cataloging-in-Publication Data
Liptak, John J., 1961–
  2012—catalyst for your spiritual awakening: using the Mayan tree of
life to discover your higher purpose / John J. Liptak.—1st ed.
      p. cm.
  ISBN 978-0-7387-1962-7
  1. Maya calendar. 2. Maya astrology. 3. Spirituality—21st century.
  4. Spiritual life—New Age Movement. 5. Two thousand twelve, A.D.
  I. Title.
  F1435.3.A8L576 2010
  529'.32978427—dc22
                                                    2009044727

Llewellyn Publications
A Division of Llewellyn Worldwide, Ltd.
2143 Wooddale Drive, Dept. 978-0-7387-1962-7
Woodbury, MN 55125-2989, U.S.A.
www.llewellyn.com

Printed in the United States of America

Contents

Introduction

Anyone paying attention to the world these days may conclude that we are racing at high speed toward a wall. Whether it be 2012, or 2036, or any date in the next fifty years for that matter, we are going to pay a price for how we've been choosing to live. Our consciousness will have to change by admitting to ourselves that we humans are soiling our own nest.

BRUCE SCOFIELD AND BARRY C. ORR IN *Mayan Astrology*

This book is written for all of the people who are afraid that the world is coming to end soon. The end of the world! Think about that phrase for a moment. At first it sounds crazy. How could the world come to an end? Yes, the latest in a long line of doomsday prophecies is rapidly closing in on us. According to Mayan calendar prophecy, December 21, 2012, will mark the end of our world from a global cataclysm. It immediately conjures up images of firestorms raining down on people, great floods sweeping people from their homes and causing massive mudslides, tidal waves crashing down on entire towns, volcanoes erupting after hundreds of years of silence, tornadoes destroying everything in their paths, and earthquakes making cracks in the earth so large that people fall into and disappear. This sounds like a made-for-television movie, doesn't it? Many New Age people who have studied Mayan Doomsday Prophecy believe the cataclysmic description above will happen on that fateful day. These researchers contend that a major reversal in the earth's magnetic field will occur and signal the end of the world as we know it.

As human beings, we inherently want to know what the future holds. Our parents always tell us to carry an umbrella in case it rains. On a larger scale, we want to know what will happen to us and that we are going to be okay. We look at prophecies not just for warnings, but also for hope, for comfort, and for a glimpse of what our lives are going to be like. Because of this need, we look to prophecies in search of a blueprint for how to live more effectively. Throughout history, civilizations around the world have tried to justify that the future is knowable and that people can prepare for catastrophic events, or they can be too inattentive, too greedy, or in too much of a hurry to see the blueprint.

An End of the World Theme

There are two different ways that the Mayan Doomsday Prophecy for December 21, 2012, is being interpreted—literally and figuratively. The literal translation of the prophecy suggests that the world will come to an end, and the human race will cease to exist. People who believe this version note that our civilization is ever-accelerating down a path toward Armageddon. To back up their theory, these believers point to the scorched-earth effects of globalization, imminent polar reversals, deforestation, war, pestilence, the depletion of the earth's fossil-fuel reserves, technological advances that make computers more important than people, rogue nations stockpiling nuclear arsenals and threatening to use them, and cities disappearing beneath flood tides. This group of people views the Mayan Doomsday Prophecy as an event of apocalyptic proportions as professed by old-age religions.

The figurative interpretation of the Mayan Doomsday Prophecy foretells quite a different scenario. People who believe this version of the prophecy suggest that on December 21, 2012, we will be in the throes of a new dawn of spiritual enlightenment. During this time, human beings will become more aware of nature and the impact that we have on nature and on the planet. In addition, human beings will begin to develop a higher intelligence, greater consciousness, and greater willingness to lead lives of service. According to this scenario, the sun will intersect with the Milky Way, causing an eclipse that will allow everyone to see the Mayan "Trees of Life." When this occurs, a new and fifth dawn of enlightenment will evolve. The Mayans and many modern "New Age" groups that study the ancient Mayans believe that the universe has been renewed four times at this point in our history. According to this belief, we have passed through four evolutions including:

- The first renewal produced animals to live on the earth with the mountains and trees.

- The second renewal produced people made from clay who could not speak or move and who eventually became insects.

- The third renewal produced monkeys.

- The fourth renewal will produce "true humans." The Mayans thought that this age defined the union of spirit and soul with matter of which the outcome was humans with mind, body, and spirit.

The Mayans believe that each previous attempt was destroyed by a certain type of cataclysm that ended the universe as it was. For the fourth renewal period ending December 21, 2012, the Mayans postulated the "end of the universe" to symbolize the coming of great change. In these changes, humankind will become more aware of their surroundings and their impact on the earth, have an increased spiritual intelligence and consciousness, and be more willing to help and serve their fellow human beings. Thus, while some sort of natural disaster cannot be ruled out, academic researchers have proposed another interpretation of the Long-Count Mayan calendar that suggests December 21, 2012, will usher in this new dawn of enlightenment and produce enlightened humans. According to this enlightenment theory, human beings have reached a point where they have become "spiritually bankrupt" and in need of enlightenment.

Academicians studying the Mayan Doomsday Prophecy suggest that the Mayan calendar is actually mapping the evolution of our innate spiritual selves. I tend to agree with this theory. I believe that the astronomically-based Mayan calendar, which will complete its first great cycle of approximately 5,200 years on December 21, 2012, is actually a map of the divine plan for humanity and its enlightenment.

I believe that this time will mark the decline of the material self and the evolution of the spiritual self. We will be evolving to the next phase of humanity in which we can experience enlightenment and experience extended spiritual oneness with a higher power. Although not the end of the world in a literal sense, it will mark the transcendence of the world as we know it. With this evolutionary change, we will begin to awaken to a more harmonious state of being in which we use all of our special "gifts" for the good of humanity and the well-being of our planet, rather than for making money and gaining power. The planet will prepare to create a new life form that is spiritually enlightened and service based.

Opportunity Beyond 2012

The December 21, 2012, date is a metaphor for a psychological end of time as we know it, summoning in a new age of spiritual renewal and rebirth. Rather than money and power, spirituality will be at the forefront of our consciousness, and people will seek Extended Spiritual Experiences, enlightenment, liberation from the barriers of their psychological minds, and transcendence of their physical bodies and egos. People will be drawn to live more authentic lives that reflect their Personal Energy Patterns and Spirituality Types. This new awareness of how to most effectively use the energy flowing inside you will probably change your interests and introduce goals and dreams that you have had but have been reluctant to act on.

That's what this book is about—enlightenment, liberation, and transcendence. This book is about thriving—not merely surviving—in this new era of spiritual seeking and enlightenment. It provides you with a roadmap for discovering your Personal Energy Pattern and Spirituality Type, and then using this information to live a life filled with many Extended Spiritual Experiences.

Thank you for allowing this book to be your guide through the evolution from a materialistic age to a spiritual one. I have been studying the ancient Mayan civilization for many years, and the people who have predicted that the forthcoming transition also tell us how to survive and thrive in this new spiritual era. The secret is to use the Mayan Tree of Life to help you learn more about yourself and others, identify your true spiritual calling, and begin having more Extended Spiritual Experiences. Think of December 21, 2012, as an opportunity that comes from crises—an opportunity for you to find, discover, explore, or reclaim spirituality in your life.

Change?

You should keep in mind that with change can come a degree of stress. Remember that December 2012 will bring the death of many old habits and a chance to integrate new, more fulfilling habits. People, however, grow at different speeds, so you should not rush your progress by comparing yourself with others. This new evolution will require you to acquire new ideas, skills, and behaviors that coincide with your Personal Energy Pattern and Spirituality Type. You should not be afraid of this new age of spirituality, but see it as a golden opportunity to bring balance to your life, career, health, and relationships.

As you begin to read about, reflect on, and assimilate information provided by the Mayans, the Mayan spirituality system described in this book will become a powerful tool that guides you on your spiritual journey beyond 2012. The process will allow you to truly feel empowered and energized in the upcoming spiritual age. Even when times seem most difficult, Mayan spirituality can act as a reference point to center your life, then propel you toward self-actualization and the fulfillment of your unique destiny. By clearing the way to have Extended Spiritual Experiences, you will bring new meaning and purpose to your life. You will also begin making decisions based on what will give you energy or take energy away.

How to Use This Book

You might begin to think about what will happen in 2012, as the start of something new. People are beginning to notice changes within themselves and within the world. Once 2012 arrives, you will begin to feel even more attuned to nature and aware of the natural cycles around you. You will also begin to be more aware of the energy that courses through your body and the bodies of others.

The heart of this book consists of practical tools and techniques to enhance your sense of energy and spirituality and to ensure that you begin having Extended Spiritual

Experiences. You will learn how the underlying principles of the Mayan Tree of Life can be applied within the context of contemporary culture and society. Then you will receive detailed information about the five Personal Energy Patterns, the twenty Spirituality Types, and the forces that are potential Influencers of the specific Spirituality Types.

The Mayan Tree of Life spirituality system presumes that all people are fundamentally happy, good, and intelligent people of varying energy patterns. When you discover, accept, and learn how to effectively use your basic Personal Energy Pattern, you can live more fully and begin to engage genuinely with every aspect of your life. Knowing about the Mayan Tree of Life and the Personal Energy Patterns is only the beginning of your journey. To experience their full enlightening power, you will need to explore them and refine your ability to apply them in your life, your relationships, and your career.

You need to remember that your Personal Energy Pattern and Spirituality Type are not fixed entities (like fate), but are maps you can use to start understanding yourself and make positive spiritual changes. In essence, they are the base from which you will continue to grow and evolve spiritually—they allow you to explore what has occurred in the past, accept yourself in the present, and plan purposefully and strategically for the future. You will be encouraged to put your past into perspective and better understand your emotions, rational and irrational thinking patterns, and behaviors.

I encourage you to not only read this book, but also experience it. By that I mean that I hope you reflect on what you read, complete the journaling questions, and practice the experiential exercises. At first, the Personal Energy Patterns and Spirituality Types will be somewhat conceptual and nebulous. Then, as the information sinks in, you will begin to feel that the Personal Energy Patterns and Spirituality Types are becoming a part of you and your identity, and you will begin to intuitively use them as your centering point. I also hope that you will analyze the events of your life in terms of your personal patterns of energy and then learn from this analysis about the nature of your reactions to the changing patterns of energy that you encounter in the world around you. Finally, you will psychologically and physically integrate the Personal Energy Patterns and Spirituality Types so that you begin having more Extended Spiritual Experiences.

Basic Premises

What you will explore in this book is grounded in the following fundamental understandings for living more effectively:

- Energy is common to all people and is vital to existence.

- By becoming familiar with the five Personal Energy Patterns and twenty Spirituality Types, you will be opening the door to a more spiritual level of being.

- Energy can best be experienced, not understood intellectually.

- We each have a different Personal Energy Pattern, Spirituality Type, and set of Influencers that guides our thoughts, feelings, and actions.

- By living according to the strengths of our Spirituality Type, we can have many Enhanced Spiritual Experiences.

- When we are blocked from living according to our Spirituality Type, we will begin to experience an imbalance that leads to stress, mental illness, and physical illness.

- To become more energetically well, we must work directly to increase our type of energy.

- Theoretical knowledge about the Mayans and their spirituality system will help you to understand your Personal Energy Pattern and how to apply it to your own life.

Organization of the Book

The book is arranged so that you can easily understand the Mayan Tree of Life Spirituality System and understand your Spirituality Type and how to use your Type to generate Extended Spiritual Experiences. Chapter 1 helps you start learning more about Mayan spirituality and contains the assessment forms you will complete to help you identify your Personal Energy Pattern and specific Spirituality Type. Chapter 2 explores the unique nature of Mayan spirituality. I'll present a framework—the Mayan Tree of Life—for exploring the true nature of your spirituality. This chapter will take a closer look at the Mayan Doomsday Prophecy, explore Mayan spirituality, and propel you on a journey to find your spiritual calling.

Chapters 3 through 7 examine the five global Personal Energy Patterns that mirror the Mayan Tree of Life, and explore the twenty unique Mayan Spirituality Types. These chapters will describe each Energy Pattern, describe behaviors that support spiritual experiences, identify primary methods for evoking spiritual experiences, and define the four Spirituality Types contained within each Energy Pattern.

Chapters 8 and 9 describe the era of spiritual bankruptcy that we have been, and are currently, experiencing and provides a method for having more Extended Spiritual Experiences in your life.

Chapters 10 and 11 help you to harness what the Mayan people called *Coyopa*, or "lightning in the blood." After showing you how to harness the energy that is inside your body, these chapters demonstrate how to use that energy to live with Extended Spiritual Experiences. Included are unique exercises that help you connect with and activate all of your unique types of energy.

The conclusion helps tie all of the materials together and prepare you for your journey to 2012 and beyond.

A Companion

Remember that life is a spiritual journey that is ultimately linked to the pursuit of personal growth and development. The Mayan Tree of Life offers you the opportunity to achieve a greater sense of harmony, add meaning to your life, enhance how you look at the world and its people, induce Extended Spiritual Experiences in your life, and better understand how you sense the world in general and why you behave in certain ways. Let this book be your companion as you prepare for and live through the "spiritual age" coming on December 21, 2012.

Getting Started

Energy is the vibrant aspect of being—the quality, texture, ambience, and tone of both the animate and the inanimate, the visible and the invisible. It is the basic vitality of our existence. It pervades our inner, psychological world as well as the outer, phenomenal world. It exists in what we see, smell, taste, touch, hear, and feel. People express their energy through attitudes, emotions, decisions, and actions. Furthermore, we each display energy in our own unique way—through body posture, facial expressions, mannerisms, word choices, the tone and tempo of our voice.

IRINI ROCKWELL IN *The Five Wisdom Energies*

Identifying and utilizing your Personal Energy Pattern and Spirituality Type will get you in the best frame of mind to meet any challenges in the new age of enlightenment. Doing so will subconsciously gear you up for an age when the spirit of humanity shifts to a higher pattern and form. By preparing for this shift, you will easily free yourself from the grips of modern materialism to embrace enlightenment and liberation. First, let's take a look at who the Mayan people are and how they came to make such bold predictions about the end of the world.

Who Are the Maya?

The Mayan people were well versed in many diverse subjects including mathematics, astronomy, and religion. Thus, their claims about a new day for all people dawning on December 21, 2012, have received worldwide attention from some of the most respected scientists all over the world. Since the first trip that my wife and I took to Mexico, I have been fascinated by this civilization and have gone back many more times to find out more about these remarkable people. The ancient Mayan civilization in its Classical period rivaled many of the greatest civilizations throughout history as well as many of our modern-day civilizations. The Mayan culture has been traced by archeologists as far back as to about 1500 BC and seemed to really flourish between 600 and 900 AD. The Maya are an American Indian group related to the inhabitants of Mexico and Central America, as well as to the American Indian populations of North and South America. They inhabited, and still inhabit to some degree, the Yucatan Peninsula of Mexico, Belize, Guatemala, the western areas of Honduras and El Salvador, and parts of the Mexican states of Tabasco and Chiapas.

The Maya were both very simplistic, yet very sophisticated. They have been credited with many artistic, mathematical, and scientific achievements. The Maya were a very innovative people and have been called the "Greeks of the New World" because many of their achievements rivaled those of ancient Athens. They developed, among other things, hieroglyphic writing, sophisticated architectural layouts, pottery, and temple-style pyramids. As can be seen from their many inventions and innovations, they were a very intellectual and scholarly people. Although the great Mayan empire began to disappear about 900 AD due to insufficient food resources, disease, and invasion by outsiders, the Mayan astrology system continues to be a source of knowledge for many spiritual seekers.

The Maya were so interested in astronomy and astrology that they had two methods for observing the stars for spiritual services: divination and prophecy. They believed that December 21, 2012, would bring an end to the world as we now know it, as well as an opportunity for all people to embrace a new way of living—a more spiritual way. The Maya have alerted all of humanity that our biological process is transforming, and we will see a return to an intuitive way of living, a heightened spiritual awareness, and a return to a self-reflective consciousness.

The Mayan astrology system is linked to the Mayan calendar, and both are profoundly correlated with the process of liberation and enlightenment. The Mayan calendar is based on the astrological cycle called the Procession of the Equinoxes, and their belief system is an outgrowth of the calendar. This mystical belief system—similar to that of the Sumerians, Egyptians, Cherokees, and Tibetans—contains an understanding of the universe and a plan that charts humanity's path toward spiritual enlightenment. The Mayan calendar, based on principles of the Mayan Tree of Life, provides a temporal framework for bringing collective enlightenment to humanity through the identification and utilization of general Personal Energy Patterns and specific Spirituality Types. The benefit of learning this new framework is that it provides, in these times of great uncertainty, navigational assistance and a lens through which you can look much deeper into yourself, come to know the purpose and meaning that each moment holds for you, and live with as many Extended Spiritual Experiences as possible.

Before we begin exploring the Mayan Tree of Life as a framework for spiritual enlightenment in greater detail, you need to take some time and explore your primary Personal Energy Pattern and the Spirituality Type that guides your thoughts, feelings, and behaviors. There are many different ways to accomplish this. In this book, you will have the opportunity to identify your Spirituality Type by completing an assessment called "What's My Spirituality Type?" This assessment, beginning on the next page, will help you to learn more about yourself and probably enhance your understanding of other people. Take some time now to complete the assessment that follows.

What's My Spirituality Type?

Remember, your Spirituality Type will provide you with information about how you feel, think, and behave. In addition, your Type provides critical spirituality information you can use to choose an enlightened occupation, communicate effectively and get along with other people, and live an enlightened life of service. After you identify your primary Spirituality Type, you will be well on your way in preparing yourself for the enlightened age that is upon us.

Instructions: Before you read about the various Spirituality Types, please complete the following assessment. The assessment was developed to help you learn more about your spiritual self and identify ways to begin having Extended Spiritual Experiences in your daily life. Keep in mind that this is not a test. Since there are no right or wrong answers, do not spend too much time thinking about your answers. Be sure to respond to every statement that follows. Read each of the statements and decide how much the statement is descriptive of you:

> If the statement is **Very Much Like Me**, write a **2** in the space next to that statement.
>
> If the statement is **Somewhat Like Me**, write a **1** in the space.
>
> If the statement is **Not Like Me**, write a **0** in the space.

1. I feel like my mission in life is to help other people	2

In the above example, the statement was **Very Much Like** the person completing the assessment. Now complete all of the items that follow.

SERVICE

PERSONAL ENERGY PATTERN

2 = Very Much Like Me   1 = Somewhat Like Me   0 = Not Like Me

1. I feel like my mission in life is to help other people   2
2. I do not like change in my life   0
3. I consider myself a warrior or crusader   2
4. I am good at resolving conflicts   2
5. I like helping people in the community   1
6. I am a leader in the community   0
7. I am interested in social reform   2
8. I am interested in peace and harmony in the world   2
9. I am attuned to the suffering of others   2
10. I like mentoring and guiding others   2
11. I quickly take sides and take action in a conflict   0
12. I stick up for the "underdog" in life   2
13. I am sensitive to the problems of others   2
14. I like to help people reach their full potential   2
15. I like to dedicate myself to causes   1
16. I feel sorrow when people or animals are mistreated   2
17. I am caring and generous toward others   2
18. I play a parental role in my family and/or community   2
19. Some people feel like I am argumentative   0
20. I hate to see conflicts between people or nations   2
21. Service to others gives me my identity   2
22. I am down-to-earth and nurturing   2
23. I am not afraid to speak out against injustice   2
24. I will fight for the causes of those who cannot fight   2

TOTALS   11   8   7   12

ROAD   CORN   FLINT   STORM

BUSINESS
PERSONAL ENERGY PATTERN

2 = Very Much Like Me   1 = Somewhat Like Me   0 = Not Like Me

1. I strive toward goals with clear and focused power — 1
2. I do well in challenging situations — 2
3. I am self-reliant and strong — 2
4. I work hard and know how to get things done — 2
5. I thrive on competition — 0
6. I always come out on top — 2
7. I can recognize and utilize the gifts of others — 2
8. I take charge and meet challenges head on — 2
9. I relentlessly go after what I want — 1
10. I am motivated to achieve success and wealth — 2
11. I like being direct and honest — 2
12. I am impatient with the incompetence of others — 1
13. I put work before leisure and relationships — 0
14. I have a strong desire to become wealthy and successful — 1
15. I am direct and tell people what I think — 2
16. I have lots of energy to seek uncharted opportunities — 1
17. I want control and power — 0
18. In business, I enjoy doing battle with others — 0
19. I can balance intuition and common sense — 2
20. I like to blaze new trails in business — 2
21. I am assertive in getting what I want — 2
22. I am motivated when I am told I cannot do something — 2
23. I put a lot of pressure on myself to do well — 2
24. I am strong-willed and stick up for my convictions — 2

TOTALS   4   9   12   10

EAGLE   JAGUAR   DEER   WIND

IMAGINATIVE
PERSONAL ENERGY PATTERN

2 = VERY MUCH LIKE ME   1 = SOMEWHAT LIKE ME   0 = NOT LIKE ME

1. I am creative and intuitive — 2 — 2
2. I am a dreamer — 1
3. I speak well in front of an audience — 2
4. I write very well
5. I love change — 1
6. I have a very active imagination — 2
7. I love to read — 2 — 2
8. I like to write and create things for future generations — 2
9. I often can create something from nothing — 1
10. I envision plans that others can carry out — 2
11. I can communicate ideas so that others understand them — 2
12. I often communicate through creativity (dancing, painting, etc.) — 2
13. I have an "artistic" spirituality — 1
14. I am not good at last minute details — 2
15. I am a talented storyteller — 2
16. I often create poetry or short stories — 2
17. I always see the beauty and possibilities in life — 2
18. If I see something, I can create it — 0
19. I am an inspirational speaker — 1
20. I like to write songs or musical arrangements — 2
21. I create vivid pictures in my mind — 2
22. I like to make things more beautiful — 0
23. I love speaking in front of groups or crowds — 2
24. I connect to inner power through my writing

TOTALS __11__ __10__ __7__ __11__

MONKEY   ANCESTORS   NIGHT   DEATH

UNDERSTANDING
PERSONAL ENERGY PATTERN

1. I am constantly trying to understand life and myself — 2
2. I am a lifelong learner and student — 2
3. I am considered very spiritual — 2
4. I am very emotional — 1
5. I am reflective and think a lot about life — 2
6. I love to work with ideas and hypotheses — 1
7. I often engage in spiritual practices — 2
8. I am a problem-solver — 2
9. I often feel uncomfortable in social situations — 1
10. I love debating my ideas and notions with others — 1
11. I am interested in living a balanced, compassionate life — 2
12. I want to make things work more effectively — 2
13. I always try to figure out the meaning in life — 2
14. I want to know why things are the way they are — 2
15. I am a seeker of deep sources of wisdom — 2
16. I easily understand complex situations — 2
17. People consider me philosophical — 1
18. I love to be challenged intellectually — 2
19. I am very religious — 0
20. I have a gentle, magnetic spirituality — 2
21. I often need time alone to process my thoughts & feelings — 2
22. I am quiet and value knowledge — 2
23. I am dedicated to inner development — 2
24. I am able to turn anything negative into something positive — 2

TOTALS   10   10   10   11

INCENSE   WATER   SERPENT   CROCODILE

FREEDOM
PERSONAL ENERGY PATTERN

2 = Very Much Like Me   1 = Somewhat Like Me   0 = Not Like Me

1. I like to just enjoy life — 2
2. I like to explore unknown territories — 2
3. I am interested in the "greening" of the Earth — 1
4. I enjoy balance between my work and leisure — 2
5. I am fun-loving and spontaneous — 1
6. I want to do new and exciting things — 2
7. I have a "green thumb" when it comes to gardening — 0
8. I would like to grow and build my own business — 2
9. I am lighthearted and outgoing — 1
10. I like adventuresome sports and hobbies — 1
11. I enjoy watching things grow — 1
12. I am good at building things — 0
13. I rarely let life's troubles get me down — 2
14. I love to travel — 2
15. I enjoy gardening and/or farming — 0
16. I am the master of many arts and crafts — 2
17. I am considered a "free spirit" — 2
18. I want the adrenaline rush from dangerous activities — 1
19. I enjoy outdoor activities like camping and hiking — 1
20. I enjoy seeing plants and animals grow — 2
21. I am slow and easygoing — 0
22. I seek adventure in all I do — 1
23. I enjoy doing physical labor, especially outdoors — 0
24. I can help people and organizations grow — 2

TOTALS   8   9   3   10

VULTURE   DOG   RABBIT   LIZARD

Scoring Directions

There are two easy steps for scoring the assessment you've just completed:

Step 1: For each of the four columns on the previous pages, count down and add the numbers you wrote in each of the blank spaces. At the bottom, write the totals for each of the columns in the spaces marked "Totals." Do not worry about the descriptors at the bottom of each page for now.

Then, transfer your totals from the assessment to the spaces below for each of the four Spirituality Types and add them to get the grand total for the Personal Energy Patterns:

SERVICE PERSONAL ENERGY PATTERN

Road __11__ + Corn __8__ + Flint __7__ + Storm __12__ = __38__

BUSINESS PERSONAL ENERGY PATTERN

Eagle __4__ + Jaguar __9__ + Deer __12__ + Wind __10__ = __35__

IMAGINATIVE PERSONAL ENERGY PATTERN

Monkey __11__ + Ancestors __10__ + Night __7__ + Death __11__ = __39__

UNDERSTANDING PERSONAL ENERGY PATTERN

Incense __10__ + Water __10__ + Serpent __10__ + Crocodile __11__ = __40__

FREEDOM PERSONAL ENERGY PATTERN

Vulture __8__ + Dog __9__ + Rabbit __3__ + Lizard __10__ = __30__

Which Personal Energy Pattern was highest for you? __Understanding__

What Do My Scores Mean?

Grand total scores on the assessment will range from 0 to 48. Scores can be interpreted in two ways. First, take a look at your grand total for each Personal Energy Pattern. Find out where your scores can be found on the following interpretation guide. For example, if you had a score of 18, that would be in the AVERAGE range.

Scores between 0 and 15 are in the **LOW** range and indicate that you do not have many of the Spirituality characteristics of this type. You probably will not find spiritual experiences engaging in these types of activities.

Scores between 16 and 32 are in the **AVERAGE** range and indicate that you have some of the Spirituality characteristics of this type. You may find some spiritual experiences engaging in these types of activities.

Scores between 33 and 48 are in the **HIGH** range and indicate that you have many of the Spirituality characteristics of this type. You probably will find many spiritual experiences engaging in these types of activities.

Step 2: Next, look at which of the four Spirituality Types within your highest Energy Pattern (for Service, the Spirituality Types would include Road, Corn, Flint, and Storm) that you had the highest score on. Scores will range from 0 to 12. Write your primary Spirituality Type in the space below and read about Spirituality Types before moving to the next chapter. If you have two or more scores that were identical, list them, then read the descriptions of each of the Spirituality Types and decide which one fits you the best.

My Primary Spirituality Type: _____

Step 3: You will be asked to record scores for your Influencers from the assessment you just completed. It should be noted that each Spirituality Type has inherent Influencers, but it is recommended that you look at how other high scores from the assessment might be influencing your Spirituality Type.

Spirituality Types

In the Mayan system, your Spirituality Type includes what psychologists over the centuries have called your temperament and many other things including your attitude, your emotions and how you express them, your thoughts, your decisions, and your behaviors. Your Spirituality Type, however, also includes your body postures, expressions, mannerisms, the speed at which you move, the tone of your voice, and the way you communicate with other people. Your Spirituality Type also serves as a framework for the types of occupational and recreational activities you choose.

The notion of Mayan Spirituality Types suggests that all people have a basic fundamental drive that propels us to think, feel, and act in prescribed ways. Thus, some people live for freedom to do what they want whenever they want, some live to engage in creative activities, and some live to serve others. Therefore, someone with a Service Spirituality Type will seek work and recreational activities through which they can serve other people.

The Personal Energy Patterns are used to group the twenty Spirituality Types based on common characteristics. Thus, as you can see from the table below, the Service Personal Energy Pattern will include Road, Corn, Flint, and Storm Spirituality Types. All four Spirituality Types are interested in helping and serving other people. In the remaining chapters, each of the Personal Energy Patterns and Spirituality Types will be described in detail. The following is a brief description of each Personal Energy Pattern and a list of the Spirituality Types associated with them.

Energy Patterns of the Spirituality Types

PERSONAL ENERGY PATTERNS	SPIRITUALITY TYPES
SERVICE—Service people enjoy being supportive of and helping others in need. They are caring people who feel genuine love and concern for others.	ROAD, CORN, FLINT, STORM
BUSINESS—Business people are confident and determined leaders of other people. They are innovative and work to achieve great things.	EAGLE, JAGUAR, DEER, WIND
IMAGINATIVE—Imaginative people express themselves through a variety of creative endeavors.	MONKEY, ANCESTORS, DEATH, NIGHT

PERSONAL ENERGY PATTERNS	SPIRITUALITY TYPES
UNDERSTANDING—Understanding people are bright and curious. They are students of life. They seek information and prize knowledge. They are driven to learn all they can in life.	INCENSE, WATER, CROCODILE, SERPENT
FREEDOM—Freedom people tend to be uninhibited and upbeat about life. They love variety and adventure. They are free-spirited and are prone to be great risk takers.	VULTURE, DOG, RABBIT, LIZARD

Now that you have identified your primary Personal Energy Pattern and your specific Spirituality Type, you are prepared to harness the "lightning" in your blood that allows you to have many Extended Spiritual Experiences in the new age. Remember that 2012 is an opportunity—your opportunity. The Maya believed that you have tremendous genetic potential that is probably lying dormant within you, waiting to be activated. Think of 2012 as a huge switch that will be turned on, providing you with the opportunity to activate and use your full potential.

Take advantage of this opportunity to discover and embrace your Spirituality Type and begin living according to the flow of your Personal Energy Pattern. Extended Spiritual Experiences (which we will discuss in chapter 9) are literally at your fingertips. You will never get a better chance to explore and claim the energy of your Spirituality Type than in 2012. Using this book as your guide, you will experience increased energy, better relationships, greater success on your job, and a sense of peace and purpose in life.

The next chapter will discuss in detail the Mayan Tree of Life Spirituality System, the five Personal Energy Patterns, the twenty Spirituality Types, Influencers, and ways to begin using your Spirituality Type to live more spiritually.

2

The Mayan Tree of Life

Now that we have entered the twenty-first century, the Mayan calendar has seized the public imagination, partly because it is ending soon, and partly because it just fascinates people.

BARBARA HAND CLOW IN *The Mayan Code*

On December 21, 2012, for the first time in about 26,000 years, the sun will intersect with the Milky Way in the galactic center. According to the Maya, this will mark the end of one world as we know it and be the beginning of a new world. Many consider this date to be the embodiment of the Tree of Life, a sacred symbol in many of the world's spiritual traditions. This alignment will bring changes of great proportion. Will you be ready?

The mechanics of how the Mayan calendar works and how it can be read to determine the "end of the world" as we know it is not important. (The specifics of the Mayan calendar and how it describes the evolution of consciousness is far too esoteric and way beyond the scope of this book.) What is important, however, is understanding how the Maya suggest we prepare for this upcoming spiritual evolution and the years beyond. I believe that it is important to understand the framework—the Book of Days—through which you and I will encounter and implement your spiritual calling.

DID YOU KNOW?

The Maya actually used two different calendars! The first was the Mayan daily calendar, called the Haab, which was comprised of 18 months, each 20 days long for a 360-day year. The other 5½ days were saved for religious ceremonies. The second calendar, called the Tzolkin, was the Mayan religious calendar. It was accurately based on the complete 26-day lunar phases of the moon from new moon to full moon and back again. This "sacred" calendar contains "The Long Count," which proposes the notion that doomsday is scheduled for December 21, 2012.

As stated in the introduction, the Maya are best known for their sophisticated calendar and their unique system for helping people to have as many spiritual experiences as possible. This system, the Mayan Tree of Life, if used properly, can give us more insight into ourselves and others, help us to explore our spirituality patterns, and show us how to use our spirituality characteristics more effectively and efficiently in the new spiritual age to come.

The roots of the Tree of Life go back to the early practices of the ancient Mayan people living in Mexico and Central America. The Tree of Life was represented and symbolized by the Mayan people in the shape of a "T" or as a cross. This symbol of a cross, or a tree with two limbs, represented the directions North, South, East, and West for the Mayan people (See Figure 1). Many other cultures around the world have utilized the symbol of a cross to represent the sacredness of life.

Personal Energy Patterns

For the Mayan people, psycho-spiritual energy was thought to reside in each person's body. This notion was represented by what they referred to as the Mayan Tree of Life. It was believed that the Mayan Tree of Life was the central tree through which all vital energy from within the earth traveled and through which all rain

WEST

SOUTH   CENTER   NORTH

EAST

Figure 1—Energy Sources of the Mayan Tree of Life

from the gods traveled. The Maya believed that all people experienced psycho-spiritual energy from five different focal points in the body—the Center, East, West, North, and South (See Figure 1).

These focal points were critical in that each one produces a very different type of energy. Following are descriptions of the five energy sources or directions:

- East is the direction of new beginnings and energy that gives birth to action and ideas. It is represented by sunshine, spring, flowers, and the first rays of the sun. East is symbolic of the future in both the spiritual and material worlds. Thus, its influence is related to an Imaginative Energy Pattern.

- West is the direction of things coming to an end, as when the sun sets below the Western horizon. It is represented by nightly death, leaves falling and being blown away, and transformation. West is the place of our ancestors and those who stand in support of us. Thus, its influence is related to an Understanding Energy Pattern.

- North is the direction of the sun at its zenith. It is represented by ancestral spirits who have left this world, wisdom, and knowledge acquired from our ancestors. North is symbolic of women, interpersonal relationships, and marriage. Thus, its influence is related to a Service Energy Pattern.

- South is the direction of mysterious generative power beneath the Earth that makes plants grow. It is represented by the force that gives life to all things,

> ## DID YOU KNOW?
>
> The Maya believed that every moment in time was in a state of flux and that shifting energies could be noticed in earthquakes and volcanoes, the wars people waged on each other, and in the changes in the human heart and spirit. Thus, they felt that the energy in everything was constantly transforming and evolving.

agricultural cycles, and abundance. South is symbolic of growth, mystery, and strength. Thus, its influence is related to a Business Energy Pattern.

- Center is also a direction in Mayan astrology. It is the direction from where the Tree of Life grows. It is symbolic of our "root" or our "center." It is this point from which we are free to choose our life path. Thus, its influence is related to a Freedom Energy Pattern.

The people of Mesoamerica felt that the nature of this psycho-spiritual energy in the human body was critical because although all people operated primarily from one distinct energy source, the other four sources are influencing us at all times. However, how each person accessed and directed these four "lesser" energy sources was up to the individual. Thus, they truly believed that all energy could be explored, harnessed, and eventually transformed to enhance a person's life. As a result, much of their spiritual practice was an attempt to activate and integrate various types of energy, and then direct this energy into activities representative of their values, interests, and abilities.

The Five Basic Personal Energy Patterns

The five basic Personal Energy Patterns are part of our very being, our interactions, our career choices, our business interests, and every other aspect of our material and spiritual worlds. These patterns express themselves in our emotions, our orientation to time, our beliefs, our worldview, and our Spirituality Type. Each distinct Personal

Energy Pattern incorporates spirituality characteristics and our experiences from childhood. The following descriptions illustrate the uniqueness of the five Mayan Personal Energy Patterns:

Service Energy—Service energy is displayed in activities that are supportive of and helping others in need. These activities show genuine love and concern for others and require great sensitivity, empathy, and selflessness. They include acts of compassion and nurturance.

Business Energy—Business energy is displayed in activities that show leadership and determination. These activities show confidence and the ability to lead other people and require motivation and innovation to accomplish. They include many aggressive and competitive acts.

Imaginative Energy—Imaginative energy is expressed through a variety of creative endeavors. These activities demonstrate passion and seem to be viewed through an artistic lens. They include acts of creative expression that require sensitivity, aesthetic appreciation, and individuality.

Understanding Energy—Understanding energy is expressed through curiosity and learning. These activities require people to seek information and prize knowledge, and are expressed through innate inquisitiveness and a drive to learn new things, question life and existence, and search for answers to the meaning of life. They include acts that are demonstrated by a love of thinking and knowledge.

Freedom Energy—Freedom energy is expressed through activities that have opportunies for variety and adventure. These activities, which can be seen in hobbies by people considered free-spirited and are prone to be great risk takers. They include acts that are spontaneous in nature and require a great deal of adaptability.

Energy is a fundamental drive that propels us to act in prescribed ways. The five Personal Energy Patterns are correlated with the five directions described above (See Figure 2). Thus, some people live for freedom to do what they want when they want, some live to engage in creative activities, and some live to serve others. A person's

WEST
Understanding

SOUTH   CENTER   NORTH
Business   Freedom   Service

EAST
Imaginative

Figure 2—Energy Sources and Five Personal Energy Patterns of the Mayan Tree of Life

Personal Energy Pattern is a framework through which you choose all of your work and recreational activities. Therefore, someone with a Service Energy Pattern will seek work and recreational activities through which they can serve other people. By understanding the five primary Energy Patterns, you will be better able to understand the twenty Spirituality Types.

Basic Premises of Energy

The Mayan Tree of Life (MTOL) provides us with an objective, measurable framework for understanding human behaviors, attitudes, and motivations. It allows us to accept the value of human differences and recognize cultural diversity. The MTOL empowers us to explore our unique energy patterns and spirituality characteristics and learn how to continually integrate untapped sources of energy into our basic spirituality structure. It also provides us with a system for improving interpersonal relationships, enhancing career development, defining problem-solving and conflict-resolution skills, increasing motivation, building more confident teams of employees, improving communication, and increasing life satisfaction. Basic assumptions about energy include:

- All human beings exhibit a particular Personal Energy Pattern that guides all their actions, thoughts, and behaviors.

THE MAYAN CALENDAR

The innovation that the Mayan people are probably best known for is their calendar. Through their knowledge of mathematics and astronomy, the Maya were able to calculate lunar cycles, predict heavenly events such as lunar eclipses, and develop a calendar system that was probably more exact than the calendar system we use today. Many of the Mayan day-to-day as well as speculative activities including astrology, astronomy, harvesting, marriage ceremonies, numerology, and religious ceremonies were based on this calendar.

- Energy exists in all we are and in all we do. Energy can be expressed physically, mentally, and spiritually and can affect our relationships, career, and outlook on life.

- All people exhibit different energy sources within each Personal Energy Pattern. Energy can be directed and used to reach greater states of self-actualization or misused in socially deviant ways.

- People can build and control energy and patterns of energy.

- Energy can become blocked for a variety of reasons including fear of failure, fear of disapproval, low self-esteem, unexpressed anger or frustration from the past, preoccupation with the future, or the inability to take appropriate risks.

- When we engage in activities related to our interests, values, and purpose in life, we have higher levels of energy. Therefore, Personal Energy Patterns are displayed in all of our activities.

Day Signs

In the Mayan culture, the Tree of Life represented the center of the universe around which all else revolved. It contained twenty Day Signs, which provide information about the basic twenty Spirituality Types (See table below). As you will see, each of the twenty major Spirituality Types is named after a Day Sign of the Mayan sacred calendar. The Day Signs are named after representative animals and forces of nature. For example, a person who has a Day Sign of Storm will have a Spirituality Type that is a force of nature, like a storm. While it is common to see a little bit of yourself in many of the Spirituality Types, one should stand out as being the closest match to your spirituality. This is called your Primary Day Sign.

Primary Day Signs in Mayan Astrology

Crocodile	Crocodile is a mysterious and primordial animal that sleeps beneath the surface and symbolizes the holiness of the world.
Wind	Wind blows here and there, is a source of great power, and is symbolic of the breath of life itself.
Night	Night is a place of inner darkness into which all of us must descend and is symbolic of a place where wisdom is found.
Lizard	Lizard is known for being the creator of the Earth and is symbolic of fertility and the power of growth.
Serpent	Serpent is known for its inner power and is symbolic of wisdom and cognitive abilities.
Death	Death is one of the luckiest Day Signs and is symbolic of undergoing a cosmic or spiritual transformation.
Deer	Deer is the lord of the forest and is known for expressing its power quite forcefully and directly.
Rabbit	Rabbit is a sign of the harvest and is symbolic of the greening or the ripening of the Earth.
Water	Water was intended to be collected and symbolized by creative ways to collect the water that has fallen from the skies.
Dog	Dog is associated with worldly pleasures and is symbolized by its sensual instincts.
Monkey	Monkeys are described as creators and craftspeople and are symbolized as having an artistic temperament.
Road	Road represents the spiritual path in life and is symbolized by spiritual service to society.
Corn	Corn is the pillar of society and is symbolized by leaders or staff of the community.
Jaguar	Jaguar seems to emerge from all challenges and difficulties with a smile and are symbolized by cunning.
Eagle	Eagle is a sign of passion and desire and is symbolized by motivation, strength, and strong spirit.

Vulture	Vulture is a slow, easygoing bird that is symbolized by pleasure and the material world.
Incense	Incense is associated primarily with thinking and is symbolized by reflection and visionary insight.
Flint	Flint sees the world in terms of "black or white" and is symbolized by healing and harmony.
Storm	Storm often feels like life is one long storm and is symbolized by compassion for higher causes.
Ancestors	Ancestors hold the power and spirit of all those who have gone before and are able to channel this energy into creative endeavors that will last forever.

The Maya used the Day Signs to identify the people in their society who would be farmers, negotiators, musicians, handball players, shamans, cooks, and those who would wage war. They also used the Day Signs to determine who would marry whom, when they would have coronations, and who would be astronomers. All these activities were timed based on the movements of the planets and thus were actually more like astronomy than astrology. Your Day Sign in the Mayan culture today is based on your birthday and its correlation to the sacred calendar. Thus, it is like astrology and requires a variety of complicated interpretations tied to your birth month, date, and year. The Maya actually believed that a person receives the energy and power of the animal or force of nature represented in the Day Sign name.

Spirituality Types in the Mayan System

The Mayan Tree of Life consists of a set of twenty Spirituality Types that correlate with each of the Primary Day Signs. The Mayan system teaches that you are born with a particular Spirituality Type as your primary type, which remains fairly constant throughout your life. However, you also have aspects of the other Spirituality Types within you. Then, over the course of your life, you incorporate the positive traits of various other Types in an attempt to become less one-dimensional and more balanced. This helps you to be more compassionate and understanding of different types of people.

Remember several points about the MTOL system and the Spirituality Types that are described in this book:

- You will probably not change your basic Spirituality Type, but you can alter ineffective behaviors associated with your basic Type and capitalize on the positive behaviors associated with your basic Type.

- All Spirituality Types have unique sets of strengths and weaknesses.

- No Spirituality Type is better than any of the other Types.

- All of the information you read about your Spirituality Type may not apply to you all of the time.

The following is a set of brief descriptors (See table below) for each of the twenty Spirituality Types that are correlated with the Day Signs from the Book of Days. For the purposes of the Mayan spirituality system in this book, I have decided to retain the English-language names that Kenneth Johnson used to designate the Day Signs in his book *Jaguar Wisdom*. Thus, there may be some name variations based on sources from which they are derived.

Descriptor of the Twenty Spirituality Types

Spirituality Type	Brief Description
Crocodile	Dreamer, full of mystery, visionary, influenced by the spirit of the times
Wind	Business, energy, makes things happen, capable of infinite power
Night	Verbal and written communicators, poetic, orators
Lizard	Master of all of the arts, likes outdoors and nature, passionate
Serpent	Known for deep wisdom, spirituality, cognitive powers are great
Death	Spiritual transformation, great writers and speakers, psychic gifts
Deer	Powerful, great leaders, very intense, dominating
Rabbit	Have green thumbs and are great farmers, strong links to family and culture

Spirituality Type	Brief Description
Water	Artistic vision, intuition, symbolism, use the mind to achieve goals
Dog	Sexual, family, loyalty, luxury, instinctual, sensuality
Monkey	Artistic temperament, born knower, absorbed in own creativity, esoteric
Road	Community and service to others, creates things for future generations
Corn	Productive, practical, parenting, leading, and nurturing
Jaguar	Cunning, linked with wealth, likes change
Eagle	Highly motivated and assertive businesspeople, materialistic, focused
Vulture	Sensual and loves leisure and life's pleasures, lack of motivation
Incense	Loves thinking and wisdom, reflective, directed action
Flint	Warriors and crusaders, always involved in conflicts, argumentative
Storm	Drawn to higher causes, sensitive, compassionate
Ancestors	Communicates through artistic endeavors

Influencers

Although one Day Sign may dominate your Spirituality Type, nobody is one pure Type. Everyone is a unique combination of their Primary Day Sign and four adjacent types from the Mayan calendar, which are naturally referred to in the Mayan Tree of Life system as Influencers. While your Primary Day Sign tends to dominate your overall Spirituality Type, Influencers can have (maybe even should have!) a significant influence on how you express your Type. These Influencers can complement or detract from the overall intensity of your spirituality.

To better understand your total spirituality, you need to explore the effect these Influencers have on your Primary Spirituality Type. For example, if you are a Corn Spirituality Type and are not very "influenced" by any of the business qualities, you

Western
Influencer

Southern   SPIRITUALITY   Northern
Influencer   TYPE   Influencer

Eastern
Influencer

Figure 3—The Influence of other Spirituality Types

may be an even more effective Corn by developing the business side of yourself. Thus, Influencers, or the development of Influencers, can positively enhance your Spirituality Type. The impact that these Influencers have on your spirituality will vary depending on your scores from the assessments in this book. Also, don't forget to look at the influence of other high scores. Although not official Influencers, you should think about ways to incorporate them into your Spirituality Type.

In the MTOL Spirituality System, Influencers represent biological and environmental forces that affect your basic Spirituality Type throughout your life. Your spirituality may blend into or be influenced by the other four Types (See Figure 3). It is important for you to explore in great detail how the other Spirituality Types associated with your Primary Type are altering your thoughts, feelings, and behaviors. In addition, you will also want to explore ways you can use these Influencers to change ineffective behaviors and live a more satisfying, productive life.

The Tree of Life suggests that all people are born with one Primary Day Sign and thus one dominating Spirituality Type. However, you can learn to modify the spirituality characteristics associated with your Spirituality Type to better use your natural talents, communicate more effectively with other people, get involved in more energizing work and leisure activities, become more balanced, and cope more effectively with stressful situations. By working with the Mayan Tree of Life spirituality system contained in this book, you can develop a deeper understanding of yourself and others, identify and break free from behavioral patterns that are ineffective in your daily life and work, and prepare yourself for the spiritual evolution in 2012.

3

Service Personal Energy Pattern & Spirituality Types

Human consciousness is rapidly transitioning to a new state, a new intensity of awareness that will manifest as a different understanding, a transformed realization, of time and space and self.

DANIEL PINCHBECK IN *2012: The Return of Quetzalcoatl*

If you have the Service Personal Energy Pattern, you care about people and like to alleviate the suffering of others. You like giving of yourself, your time, and your resources. You are sensitive to the feelings of others and like being supportive. You are inclined to be a self-sacrificing, caring, and compassionate person with a strong desire to serve others. Your mission in life is to remain selfless and give more than you take. You feel genuine love and concern for others and helping others makes you feel worthwhile.

Behaviors That Support Spiritual Experiences	Behaviors That Hinder Spiritual Experiences
• Caring	• Nonassertive
• Loving	• Sensitive
• Intuitive	• Shy
• Understanding	• Withdrawn
• Compassionate	• Gullible
• Gentle	• Rebellious
• Positive	• Conservative
• Friendly	• Deliberate
• Generous	• Radical
• Patient	• Obsessive
• Helpful	• Righteous

Primary Characteristics of Service Spirituality Types

Your willingness to help others best enables you to have Extended Spiritual Experiences. Service-oriented individuals tend not to get upset in a crisis—in fact, you thrive during times of crisis. Your aim is to be liked and keep harmony among people, places, and things. You are a good listener and often let others initiate conversations. You tend to trust what others say and do. The following list describes characteristics of Service Spirituality Types. Check off the items that are true for you:

☐ Prefer to listen than talk

☐ Take my time

☐ Do not like criticism

☐ Avoid confrontation

☐ Do not like to be the center of attention

☐ Speak up when it is appropriate

☐ Look people directly in the eye

☐ Love to help others

☐ Feel the pain of others

☐ Believe that service is the ultimate way of helping

☐ Want to make the world a better place

☐ Is idealistic

☐ Service is spiritual for me

Occupations and Leisure Activities

People with a Service Personal Energy Pattern are well-suited for many different types of activities. You love doing things for others and look for opportunities to bring other people happiness and success. Selflessness is your guiding life and career philosophy. The following is a list of some occupations and leisure activities that will be satisfying for you and might lead to Extended Spiritual Experiences:

OCCUPATIONS

In the list that follows, place an X in the box in front of occupations that you think might bring you Extended Spiritual Experiences:

Supporting/Teaching

☐ Teacher—middle school, elementary school, high school

☐ Special education teacher

☐ Teacher's aide

☐ Education administrator

Counseling

☐ Social worker

☐ Parole officer

☐ Mental-health worker

☐ Child welfare caseworker

☐ Child-care worker

☐ Clergy member

☐ Community service manager

☐ Counselor

☐ Psychologist

Health/Wellness

☐ Emergency medical technician

☐ Music therapist

☐ Nurse

☐ Recreational therapist

☐ Physical therapist

☐ Dietitian

☐ Home economist

FREE-TIME ACTIVITIES

In the list that follows, place an X in the box in front of leisure activities that you think might bring you Extended Spiritual Experiences:

☐ Mental-health volunteer

☐ Learning sign language

☐ Special Olympics volunteer

☐ Human rights organizations

☐ Camp counselors

☐ Church activities

- ☐ Mentoring others

- ☐ Volunteering in a homeless shelter

- ☐ Tutoring

- ☐ Fighting for causes

- ☐ Helping in an elderhostel

- ☐ Designated driver program

- ☐ Neighborhood watch groups

- ☐ Consumer protection groups

- ☐ Big Brother/Big Sister volunteer

- ☐ Helping others learn English

Service Personal Energy Pattern

The Service Personal Energy Pattern is comprised of the following four Spirituality Types:

ROAD	CORN
Profound need to help other people, caring and compassionate server, attuned to the suffering of others, wants to positively impact the lives of others, selfless servant, willing to make personal sacrifices for others, emotional, empathetic.	Leader in the community, down-to-earth, practical, nurturing, helps people realize their full potential, mentor, guide, leader for service organizations, wants to make the world a better place to work and live.
FLINT	STORM
Represents social standards, morals, and values of society, speaks out about injustices, interested in reform, argumentative, interested in improving things, strong belief in convictions, relentless in the pursuit of justice, radical.	Interested in peace and harmony, resolves conflicts, cheers people up, supportive, stands up for the underdog, idealist, balanced, fighter, diplomatic, charming, intuitive, great psychological insight.

In the next section, each Spirituality Type within the Service Personal Energy Pattern is described in greater detail. Make note of the strength of this Type and the Influencers for you.

Road Description

Road is a symbol of great energy and power that can propel you along life's path, or the "Road of Life." You are endowed with power, but employ this power in unassuming ways. With a keen interest in helping and working in your community, you live a quiet life of service to others. This service often takes the form of spiritual service, but may also be accomplished through artistic vocations, counseling, teaching, and medicine.

You have a profound drive to help other people in need and are proud to provide caring and compassionate service. This selfless service, in return, provides you with a sense of great meaning and purpose in life. You receive spiritual and emotional rewards from the service you provide to other people. By helping others you are able to fully realize who you are as a human being.

Your compassion for others stems from being highly attuned to the pain and suffering of other people, in part, due to the awareness of your own pain. This fuels your mission even further. Whenever you notice that anyone or anything needs help or is hurting, you will use all of the resources at your disposal to help fix the problem. Ultimately, you want to make an impact on other people's lives and make the world a better place to live.

The drive to help others is so great that it seems like you are on a personal crusade. However, you mustn't let your attempts to take care of others prevent you from attending to your own needs. You are at your finest when you use your strength and compassion to help others find their inner strength to solve their own problems.

As an extremely gentle and caring individual, you have the ability to understand the feelings of other people and empathize with what they need and feel. You are quite willing to make personal and professional sacrifices to help and heal others less fortunate than you, and are so compassionate that you often lend a helping hand to strangers. You love all people equally and are willing to help others without questioning the reasons and their motives.

For you, self-sacrifice is a spiritual act. Due to your great need to be involved with things greater than yourself, you are able to transcend many of your own needs—sacrificing your own comfort, money, and material possessions—to work to benefit others. Often, you feel like you have to give up everything you value to be a good and caring person. As you see it, your mission in life is to give completely of yourself to help others in need. This selfless service is uplifting and allows you to feel a sense of self-actualization and self-satisfaction.

You are very emotional yourself, which enables you to quickly establish a connection with other people. With a natural intuition that helps you to understand and identify with those around you, reaching out to others with tremendous compassion and empathy is second nature. Because of this ability to naturally feel and sense what others are feeling, you often find yourself experiencing a wide range of emotions.

One problem associated with the intense level of the feelings you experience is that you often get hurt easily. Although you are able to learn from each of these experiences, the hurtful acts or words from others can make you feel very bad, and this hurt tends to last for long periods of time. When this happens, you usually are able to recover by focusing your energies on other people less fortunate than yourself.

You also adjust easily to change and are able to go with the flow. Then you can easily sense what is present and what is needed in a situation so that you can connect with the people and help them. Thus, you use your intense feelings to connect with others and actually feel what they are feeling. You may even know things intuitively before they happen.

You love giving of yourself and are driven to do so. Service gives you a sense of identity in your life. As long as you feel you have people to help, you feel worthwhile and content. Persistent and dedicated in your efforts, you will actually go out of your way to find people to help. Your greatest feelings of joy come from the selflessness you feel when assisting others. When you are able to help people in your occupation, you will work very hard. You may even become obsessed or too involved with the

> ### SHERRY
>
> Sherry is a typical Road Spirituality Type. She really cares about others and sincerely wants to help them succeed. A social worker for a social service agency in her city, she counsels people receiving public assistance and helps them find employment, child care, housing, and transportation. Because she really cares about the welfare and well-being of her clients, she also ensures that her clients have enough to eat and are medically and psychologically healthy. Sherry receives a great deal of inner satisfaction from directly helping other people. Rather than simply providing clients with resources, she tries to teach them how to be more self-sufficient so they will not need her services. Points of emphasis include dealing more effectively with issues in their everyday lives, dealing with relationships, and solving personal and family problems. Sherry has been known to assist families with serious domestic problems—even situations that involve spouse abuse and child abuse. Sherry also enjoys helping seniors and often runs support groups for people who are caregivers of the elderly.

people you are trying to help. You just want to express your greatest gift—service to other people less fortunate than yourself.

Finding Your Primary Influencers for Road

Look back at the assessments that you completed in the introduction. The Road Spirituality Type has four primary Influencers: Lizard, Ancestors, Death, and Flint. On the chart that follows, write the scores for each of the four Influencers on the line next to that name. The highest score is the greatest influence in your life. You should then make note of how that Influencer is affecting your current Spirituality Type and work to integrate aspects of the other Influencers.

Lizard = _____

Death = _____   ROAD   Flint = _____

Ancestors = _____

Lizard

Lizard spirituality traits influence you by pushing you to bring life to and cultivate whatever is around you or available to you. You get tremendous satisfaction from making living things, people, and organizations grow and eventually prosper. How you choose to do this largely depends on your interests and the available resources in your life and community. You could choose to cultivate endeavors such as raising a child or children, tending to your garden, starting and growing your own business, leading an existing business to greater heights, or developing solutions to social problems. If Lizard is Sherry's primary Influencer, she might try to start a business incubator to help her clients start their own businesses. Lizard will influence you to help things and people grow and develop. You need to become aware of the things in your life and your community that you have an interest in seeing grow and prosper.

What do you want to cultivate or bring to life?

_____

_____

_____

Ancestors

Ancestors spirituality traits influence you to use your ability to dream and use your imagination to visualize opportunities for yourself and others. Ancestors pushes you to imagine things that ordinary people cannot even imagine. You believe that if you can see something, then you can create it or make it possible. If Ancestors is Sherry's primary Influencer, she might try to develop a process by which her clients could receive their benefits easier. Ancestors will influence you to use your imagination to dream of and then create opportunities for yourself and people in your life. You need to take time to let your imagination do its creative work developing an opportunity and then you work to make it a reality.

What types of opportunities do you visualize for people less fortunate than you? How will you work to make this visualization a reality?

_____

_____

_____

Death

Death spirituality traits influence you to harness your passion and make contributions through creative expression, particularly writing. You feel fulfilled, content, and one with the universe when you are creating things and are driven to express your creativity. Whatever artistic projects you get involved with, you are passionate and tend to excel in activities such as entertaining, writing, drawing, painting, designing, and cartooning. If Death is Sherry's primary Influencer, she might try art-therapy techniques to make her clients feel more comfortable talking about their issues and problems. Death will influence you to use your expressive and writing skills to help you and others excel in their work. You should work to enhance your writing skills, or other artistic talents, by taking courses at a local college. Consider going into an occupation in which you are able to integrate artistic talents.

How are you creative? How can this creativity help you complete your spiritual mission?

_____

_____

_____

FLINT

Flint spirituality traits influence you to be a leader in the community. You believe that you represent the social standards, morals, and values of society and often feel like the voice for other people, especially those less fortunate than yourself. Because of your interest in uncovering conspiracies and wrongdoing about a variety of social issues, you will gladly speak out about any injustices you uncover in society. You are very committed to causes you believe in. If Flint is Sherry's primary Influencer, she would e-mail members of the senate and congress in her city to provide better standards for people with whom she works. Flint will influence you to take up the cause for others who cannot defend themselves. You are an activist whose voice must be heard and who will gain tremendous satisfaction by being a civic leader, and maybe even running for political office.

What causes would you like to fight for? How can you be a voice for other people less fortunate than you?

_____

_____

_____

Corn Description

Corn is a symbol of great productivity and accomplishment. Therefore, you often become leaders in your communities. You either have many children in your family or you play a parental role for your extended families or people in your community.

> ## JAMES
>
> James is a typical Corn Spirituality Type. He works as the director of a nonprofit organization that helps people who have psychological and physical disabilities. James is responsible for ensuring that the services are being provided properly and coordinates all of the training for volunteers of the organization. Training volunteers who can then turn around and make a difference to the people being served in the community by his nonprofit organization is a source of tremendous satisfaction for James. Many of the organization's clients are attempting to find ways to increase their capacity to live independently. James believes that he has talents in providing rehabilitation counseling services for the clients, but he also knows that he can make a much greater difference in their lives as an innovative nonprofit director. In this capacity, he can train people who can then train others and, hopefully, help even more people. Feeling a sense of responsibility for the well-being of everyone in his community, James even spends some of his weekends volunteering at the local Boys and Girls Club.

In general, you are down-to-earth, practical, and nurturing. However, you tend to be very conservative and have a tendency to become complacent. You do not like much change in your life or your career. Like people with a Road Spirituality Type, you are not interested in the limelight or in accolades for your productivity and your accomplishments.

You are compelled to express yourself through a sense of duty and responsibility to be supportive to whomever and whatever you value. With a deep sense of caring and compassion for others, you want to see other people make the most out of their lives. You thrive on helping other people realize their full potential. Therefore, you do what you can to help mentor and guide others to make good choices and achieve greater success. You enjoy fostering their interests and talents, so that they in turn are prepared to make a difference in society.

Often assuming responsibility for the well-being of society and the social order, you provide pathways and frameworks through which other people can thrive and self-actualize. The services you provide are designed to contribute to, and support, your family, community, and society so that its members can achieve greater success and satisfaction.

You are very willing to accept leadership roles, whether for pay or as a volunteer, in agencies and organizations in which you can provide services to others. By calling on the wisdom you have derived from your own life experiences, you are able to counsel others. However, your greatest strength may be your ability to help other people see and understand the big picture in life, and then see how their behavior fits into that picture. You have the ability to see what needs to be done, or what possibly can be done, to make the world a better place in which to work and play.

Finding Your Primary Influencers for Corn

Look back to the assessments that you completed in the introduction. The Corn Spirituality Type has four primary Influencers: Serpent, Crocodile, Deer, and Storm. On the chart that follows, write the scores for each of the four Influencers on the line next to that name. The highest score is the greatest influence in your life. You should then make note of how that Influencer is affecting your current Spirituality Type.

Serpent = _____

Deer = _____   CORN   Storm = _____

Crocodile = _____

SERPENT

Serpent spirituality traits influence you to express yourself through activities in which you can tap into a more divine awareness and share these experiences with other people. You are able to transcend the matters of this Earth in many spiritual ways including religion, mystical experiences, and the teachings of various spiritual figures. If Serpent is James's primary Influencer, he would ensure that religious and spiritual wellness was a part of the services provided by his nonprofit organization. Serpent influences you to seek the spiritual in your everyday life, regardless of your religious orientation. You will probably find great satisfaction in learning about, reading about, and applying ancient spiritual and philosophical teachings into your occupation.

How can you use transcendental or spiritual/religious experiences to help other people?

_____

_____

_____

CROCODILE

Crocodile spirituality traits influence you toward the mysterious side of life and an interest in the more esoteric aspects of human nature and human development. You thrive on exploring the mysteries or hidden aspects of those things or people in which you are interested. In reality, you are a problem-solver in that you enjoy using your penetrating intelligence to discover things that you feel could be working more effectively and then using your strategic skills to improve the situation. If Crocodile is James's primary Influencer, he might consider doing a research study to try and identify the factors that contribute to the psychological illnesses of some of his clients. Crocodile influences you to look deeply into the mysteries of human nature and come up with theories that you can apply in your work. You will probably find great satisfaction in reading about and practicing spiritual traditions other than your own, exploring New Age self-help programs like the Enneagram, learning about ancient mystical practices, and becoming more involved with divination.

In what ways can you make other people's lives more valuable?

_____

_____

_____

Deer

Deer spirituality traits influence you to be quite forceful and direct. You have a tendency to dominate most situations, which is why you can become a civic leader. Whether for worldly or spiritual purposes, you come on very strong with a great deal of power. You make a great leader because you have vision, trust in yourself, trust in your knowledge, and the ability to get things done. If Deer is James's primary Influencer, he might organize a rally in front of the courthouse to demand more money for people with mental and physical disabilities. Deer influences you to use your organizational and leadership skills to help those who may not be able to help themselves. You have natural leadership qualities and other people tend to follow you and listen to what you say. Find ways to use these leadership skills on the job or in your spare time.

How can you acquire the traits to become a civic leader?

_____

_____

_____

Storm

Storm spirituality traits influence you to capitalize on your intense compassion and energy to fight battles for higher causes. You tend to be very compassionate, and your sensitive temperament allows you to better serve the world. You are able to do naturally whatever needs to be done to bring people and things in society together in peace and harmony. If Storm is James's primary Influencer, he might dedicate some of his spare time traveling to other countries to help them set up nonprofit programs like his. Like a Storm, you are a force of nature that other people need to reckon with. Remember that you are most passionate when you have a cause to fight for. You should think about the causes that upset you the most and then develop a plan to use your intense energy to make that situation better.

What cause or causes would you like to dedicate yourself to?

_____

_____

_____

Flint Description

You believe that you represent the social standards, morals, and values of society, and often feel like you are the voice for other people, especially those who cannot argue for themselves. Because of your strong interest in uncovering conspiracies and wrongdoing in politics, journalism, and environmental issues, you will gladly speak out about any injustices you uncover in society. You are very committed to causes you believe in, willing to work patiently, yet persistently, to bring about necessary reforms, which might include such things as improving your town, initiating recycling projects, volunteering to help the homeless, rallying for a cause, or picketing to stop an injustice.

You derive your identity by working on behalf of those less fortunate. With strong opinions and convictions and a willingness to argue for your perspective, you attempt to change public policy if at all possible.

Often adopting a philosophical stance that focuses on long-range problems and concerns, you are interested in improving things in your town and in society in general. If necessary, you are willing to get your hands dirty and bring about the changes you deem necessary. You can become very critical and highly vocal about the inhumanities that you see in the world.

Because of your interest in teaching and advocating for social issues and social standards, you always stay abreast of current affairs, the environment, politics, and society at large. You can be very outspoken about social injustices and work to bring about the necessary reforms to improve society. You tend to have strong convictions and opinions, will quickly defend your position, and may even get involved in radical and extreme attempts to solve the ills of society.

Always looking for ways to make life and society a better place for others and for future generations, you never think that the quality of life on this Earth for many people is quite good enough. This makes you constantly strive to improve and reform our social system. You tend to be an idealist who strives to make order out of the chaos that fills our world.

You are continually conscious of the flaws in yourself, in others, and in the social order. This triggers your need to improve and find solutions. This need to improve things can be beneficial for others and for society, but when it turns into an obsession, it can be detrimental to your health and the well-being of others. You sincerely and wholeheartedly strive to make the world a better place. Because of your high moral principles and unwavering belief in your convictions, you are an excellent leader and can get things done. With your ability to inspire other people to follow you in your own vision of perfection, you are frequently at the forefront of a variety of reform movements.

You are driven and ambitious when it comes to reform and social justice issues—sometimes to the point of being a workaholic. You are an active and practical person who can get many things done. An active and practical person, you seem to be a natural organizer who is quite attentive to the details of a project. You are a list-maker who will find ways to accomplish every item. By nature you are industrious and reliable and tend to be the first one to arrive at work and the last one to leave.

> ### Sandy
>
> Sandy is a typical Flint Spirituality Type. He is a mental-health counselor who believes the best way to help his clients and others suffering from mental illnesses is through reforming the mental-health system. Seen as some by radical, he is extremely committed to this cause, as evidenced by his membership in the World Health Organization, attendance at rallies on Capitol Hill for improved mental-health services, and work to get members of Congress to change some of the mental-health laws. Sandy is also thinking about starting a grassroots nonprofit that would benefit members of the community who cannot afford mental-health counseling services. While he knows that making these types of changes is not easy, he is not in a hurry. Personal experience tells him that any improvements will be welcome. Sandy had a family member very negatively affected from having a mental illness and vowed never to let anyone else suffer like that, which is why he uses every opportunity he gets to inform and teach people about mental illnesses. Education about mental illness is a key component to reform, and he will not be content until significant changes are made in the mental-health system. He is also very adept at organizing publicity campaigns to influential people in politics.

This is especially true when you are in the middle of a reform movement or fighting for a social cause that is dear to your heart.

Relentless in your pursuit of justice and equality, you often have a hard time relaxing because you feel like there are so many causes for which to fight. You are very thoughtful and quite emotional, but you are known for your quick and decisive action. Getting many things done and willing to fight for just about any cause that you deem justified, you are interested in helping people through the reshaping and reconstruction of society and its social policies.

Finding Your Primary Influencers for Flint

Look back at the assessments that you completed in the introduction. Flint Spirituality Type has four primary Influencers: Dog, Death, Road, and Lizard. On the chart that follows, write the scores for each of the four Influencers on the line next to that name. The highest score is the greatest influence in your life. You should then make note of how that Influencer is affecting your current Spirituality Type.

Dog = _____

Road = _____   FLINT   Lizard = _____

Death = _____

Dog

Dog spirituality traits influence you to seek out the excitement associated with exploring and charting unknown territories. Dog pushes you to do new and exciting things, including things that no one has done before. You want to seek adventures that will test both your mental faculties as well as your physical attributes. If Dog is Sandy's primary Influencer, he might research ways that he could create a nonprofit that could come to the houses of people in need, rather than having them come to his clinic. Dog influences you to try new things and challenge your sense of who you truly are—to "think outside of the box" and to move beyond your comfort zone. By pushing the boundaries, you can discover mental, physical, social, and spiritual attributes and levels of energy that you never thought you possessed.

What unknown territories would you like to explore? How can you use adventure in your work to help others?

_____

_____

_____

DEATH

Death spirituality traits influence you to harness your passion and make contributions through creative expression, especially writing. You will feel fulfilled, content, and one with the universe when you are creating things. Therefore, your nature is to be driven to express your creativity. You find yourself excelling at most any artistic project, which may include activities such as entertaining, writing, drawing, painting, designing, and cartooning. If Death is Sandy's primary Influencer, he might work on writing an article or a book that could draw attention to the need of his clients. Death influences you to express the creative side of yourself, whether in your work or in your spare-time activities. You are a natural-born creator; you just need the opportunity and the venue to create. Think about the types of art you enjoy creating, work to hone your skills in that passion, and then apply those skills in your work.

What creative abilities do you possess that can help you in your spiritual mission?

_____

_____

_____

ROAD

Road spirituality traits influence you to use your tremendous love of other people and your interest in helping as many people as you possibly can. Highly attuned to the pain and suffering of other people, your sensitivity fuels your mission even further, though you live a quiet life of service to others. This service often takes the form of spiritual service, but may also be accomplished through artistic vocations, counseling, teaching, and medicine. If Road is Sandy's primary Influencer, he might offer pro bono counseling to people without insurance. Road encourages you to become more empathetic to the suffering of others. It allows you to move beyond your own ego, success, and suffering and put yourself in the shoes of others and understand what they are experiencing. Think about how you can use your empathy and your ability to help others make their lives more effective.

How can you best alleviate the pain and suffering of other people?

_____

_____

_____

LIZARD

Lizard spirituality traits influence you to bring to life and cultivate whatever is around you or available to you, driving you to make living things, people, and organizations grow and eventually prosper. How you choose to do this largely depends on your interests and the available resources in your life and in your community. If Lizard is Sandy's primary Influencer, he might try to cultivate a community garden where people could plant and harvest their own vegetables. Lizard influences you to find a way to make people and things grow in your life. You are a natural facilitator and gain tremendous satisfaction in seeing others grow to their full potential. Your role may be as a mentor to those who are following in your footsteps because you enjoy taking people under your wing and sharing your knowledge and understanding so that they may prosper.

What venue will you use to cultivate the people in your community or country?

_____

_____

_____

Storm Description

You are a natural at doing whatever it takes to bring people and things in society together in peace and harmony. You have a keen sense of justice and fairness and are constantly on guard to what is going on in society that seems to be off balance, immoral, or just plain wrong. When things seem wrong in your community, nation, or in society in general, you always seem to know what to say and do to help things become more balanced.

While willing to go along with others in order to keep the peace, you must guard against giving up your own agenda just to avoid conflict. You are devoted to the quest for peace—to maintain your own peace of mind, as well as working to establish harmony and peace in the world. Possessing a calm easygoing demeanor, you are able to form a deep connection with other people, which enables you to understand all sides of an issue, find a solution, and play peacemaker between two squabbling people or parties.

Besides resolving conflicts, you are also good at reducing stress in people's lives, cheering up those who are depressed, or simply providing nurturing support. Quick to jump to the side of the underdog, you are willing to stand up and openly fight against injustices in the world. You are an idealist who envisions and works to create a world in which all people are equal and are treated with the respect they deserve. However, if at all possible, you do not like to rock the boat.

You can be quite diplomatic when you need to be. By using your gift for confronting others in a non-confrontational manner, you often bring about change with your typical charming approach, intuitional abilities, psychological insights, and natural intelligence. When all this fails, however, you can get very action-oriented.

KATHY

Kathy is a typical Storm Spirituality Type who envisions a world in which all people are able to live without conflict and fighting. Taking advantage of her natural gift for seeing many different points of view and then suggesting solutions, wherever she goes, Kathy always seems to be playing the peacemaker as she hates to see conflict and disharmony between people and will do whatever is necessary to maintain peace and harmony. She hates to see any person harmed or animal mistreated, so she has made this her own personal cause. An active member of PETA, she does everything she can to ensure that animals are not harmed by human beings. Always an advocate for the underdog, she is quite willing and able to stand up against and fight any injustices she sees in the world. Kathy wants to leave a more peaceful world for her children. She is very supportive and believes that we can have a world in which all people are treated with respect, regardless of who they are and how much money they have. She is very supportive of other people, but often spends a great deal of her energy acting as a mediator between two parties. However, she has a hard time realizing how much emotional energy goes into playing the part of mediator and protector. She is the strong, silent type and takes pride in her ability to persist and endure.

You often demonstrate your commitment to peace and justice by being willing to fight for your cause and do what it takes to make life better for all people.

When you do become committed to a particular cause, you can become quite direct and authoritarian. For example, it is painful for you to see other people, animals, or things, such as the environment, mistreated. You abhor domination of any one people by another people. When you see these types of injustices, you are quick to put your unique gifts into action to bring about justice and harmony. You want other people to be less combative, a trait you possess.

Finding Your Primary Influencers for Storm

Look back at the assessments that you completed in the introduction. The Storm Spirituality Type has four primary Influencers: Monkey, Deer, Corn, and Serpent. On the chart that follows, write the scores for each of the four Influencers on the line next to that name. The highest score is the greatest influence in your life. You should then make note of how that Influencer is affecting your current Spirituality Type.

Monkey = _____

Corn = _____   STORM   Serpent = _____

Deer = _____

Monkey

Monkey spirituality traits influence you to think in terms of metaphors and analogies and to create vivid pictures in your mind. Maintaining a holistic perspective on life allows you to always look at the big picture, whether it involves a project at work, at home, or in a recreational activity. You are able to create novel applications to existing services, products, and projects. If Monkey is Kathy's primary Influencer, she might try to create an advertising campaign that helps fight against the mistreatment of animals. Monkey influences you to use your creativity to make an impact on the lives of people and animals. Adding to your effectiveness is the ability to see the big picture and not get bogged down in the day-to-day details that cause some people to procrastinate.

How can you use your creativity to help you help other people or animals?

_____

_____

_____

Deer

Deer spirituality traits influence you to be strong and resilient in your social advocacy and to be quite forceful and direct. You have a tendency to dominate most situations, which is why you can become a civic leader. Whether for worldly or spiritual purposes, you come on very strong and have a great deal of power. You make a great leader because you have vision, trust in yourself, trust in your knowledge, and the ability to get things done. If Deer is Kathy's primary Influencer, she might organize a demonstration outside of a local "puppy mill" to raise awareness of the effects of overbreeding dogs. Deer influences you to take on activities that will enhance your power and status in the community. Through social advocacy you can get what you need, whether it is spiritual power or more practical, material power. You can be quite a force of nature and can use this force to implement your vision of the way things should be in the world.

How can you best use this strength and resiliency to help others in need?

_____

_____

_____

Corn

Corn spirituality traits influence you to fight for peace and justice in your community. It prompts you to be very active in social organizations and in social leadership—often becoming a leader in your community. You either have many children in your family or you play a parental role for your extended families or the people in your community. In general, you are down-to-earth, practical, and nurturing to other people. You are compelled to express yourself through a sense of duty and responsibility to be supportive to whomever and whatever you value. If Corn is Kathy's primary Influencer, she might volunteer at the local SPCA on the weekends or foster dogs until they are adopted. Corn influences you to be extremely nurturing in whatever you do. You support other people and feel it is your duty to make things better for future generations. You take great pride in your interest in, and ability for, helping people to grow psychologically, spiritually, and emotionally.

How can you help others realize their full potential?

_____

_____

_____

Serpent

Serpent spirituality traits influence you to express yourself through activities in which you can tap into a more divine awareness and share these experiences with other people. You are able to transcend the matters of this Earth in many spiritual ways including religion, mystical experiences, and the teachings of various spiritual figures. If Serpent is Kathy's primary Influencer, she might ask a spiritual leader in her community to have a service for people's pets or provide instruction on Eastern ideas about the connectedness of all people and things. Serpent influences you to get involved in a religious or spiritual way and prompts you to study the religious, spiritual, and mystical readings of some of the great cultures throughout history, and then find a way to implement this knowledge in helping others. Some find that missionary work is an excellent way to implement this calling with a Serpent Influencer.

How can you use transcendental experiences to help other people?

_____

_____

_____

Service-oriented people feel that it is their responsibility and duty to make and leave the world a better place for generations yet to come. If you are one of these Spirituality Types, how will you work to change the world? Think about it and write several things you would like to do to help improve the world we live in:

_____

_____

_____

_____

_____

_____

_____

_____

_____

_____

_____

_____

_____

_____

_____

_____

4

Business
Personal Energy Pattern
& Spirituality Types

We're shifting from a world where we learned to use cleverness and willpower to bridge imagined gaps between ourselves and others— and get what we want—to a world where there are no bridges to cross, where love, support, the easy materialization of results, and freedom are readily at hand.

PENNEY PEIRCE IN *Frequency: The Power of Personal Vibration*

If you have the Business Personal Energy Pattern, you seek to be the best at all you do—and the first to do it. You can be spontaneous and act quickly when your interest is piqued. You are confident and determined to lead the way to completion. You are good at initiating projects and then motivating yourself and others to complete their projects. You are an innovative leader and are able to achieve great things. You seem to be constantly pursuing new achievements.

Behaviors That Support Spiritual Experiences

- Assertive
- Independent
- Decisive
- Confident
- Competitive
- Authoritative
- Ambitious
- Motivated
- Responsible
- Self-starting
- Goal-centered

Behaviors That Hinder Spiritual Experiences

- Pushy
- Domineering
- Determined
- Competitive
- Overbearing
- Controlling
- Intimidating
- Impatient
- Demanding
- Obstinate
- Sarcastic

Primary Characteristics of Business Spirituality Types

Your ability to lead others is how you are best able to have Extended Spiritual Experiences. You are a "take charge" person who tends to be very decisive, and can delegate work to other people. You lead and also expect others to follow your lead. You like being in situations where you have the opportunity for advancement and increased leadership. The following list describes characteristics of Business Spirituality Types. Check off the items that are true for you:

☐ Use logical analysis

☐ Provide directions for others

☐ Manage projects

☐ Solve problems and make decisions

☐ Direct, control, and organize

☐ Set and meet specific deadlines

☐ Schedule tasks for others

☐ Like to organize and manage people and tasks

☐ Attend to immediate and tangible tasks

☐ Provide structure and order in a business organization

☐ Evaluate others

☐ Observe and attend to details

☐ Planning and completing projects

☐ Like to be in charge

Occupations and Leisure Activities

Many different types of activities are well suited for people with a Business Personal Energy Pattern. You like to work—in school, on the job, or in your relationships. You are a workaholic who needs little motivation to produce great things. The following is a list of some occupations and leisure activities that will be satisfying for you and might lead to Extended Spiritual Experiences:

Occupations

In the list that follows, place an X in the box in front of occupations that you think might bring you Extended Spiritual Experiences:

Management

☐ Human resource manager

☐ Networking manager

☐ Management analyst

☐ Chief executive

☐ Office manager

☐ Supervisor

Business

☐ Financial planner

☐ Mortgage broker

☐ Economics analyst

☐ Insurance agent

☐ Real estate agent

☐ Sales manager

Sales

☐ Advertising agent

☐ Door-to-door sales worker

☐ Field representative

☐ Fund-raiser

☐ Buyer

☐ Retail salesperson

☐ Public relations manager

Free-time Activities

In the list that follows, place an X in the box in front of leisure activities that you think might bring you Extended Spiritual Experiences:

☐ Managing a political campaign

☐ Chairing social committees

☐ Budget planning

☐ Organizing community activities

☐ School board member

☐ Organizing neighborhood events

- ☐ Coaching youth

- ☐ Directing plays and musicals

- ☐ Fund-raising

- ☐ Public speaking

- ☐ Coordinating disaster aid programs

- ☐ Officer in an organization

- ☐ PTA president

- ☐ Planning family recreational activities

- ☐ Leading a community group

Business Personal Energy Pattern

The Business Personal Energy Pattern is comprised of the following four Spirituality Types:

EAGLE	JAGUAR
Loves power and control, driven to make an impact, likes to direct the actions of others, influential, likes status, interested in financial power, manipulative, meets challenges head-on, assertive, achiever, self-determined, focused.	Interested in vanquishing and conquering others, motivated by doing battle for power, likes to solve problems, goal-directed, winning is everything, wants control, loves being right, powerful leader, loves the rewards that go with success.
DEER	WIND
Great leader with vision, able to get things done, loyal and beloved leader, benevolent, enjoys recognition, goal-oriented, confident, direct, self-reliant, strong, takes calculated risks, enjoys giving and receiving compliments.	Natural-born leader, driven to be first, self-assured, leads by example, blazes new trails, plows through obstacles, courage, charisma, confident, inspired, motivated, energetic, imaginative.

In the next section, each Spirituality Type is described in greater detail. Make note of the strength of this Type and the Influencers for you.

Jaguar Description

You are interested in attempting to vanquish and conquer anything and everyone that challenges you and stands in your way. This sense of doing battle with people is the primary motivator in your life. When presented with problems to solve and obstacles to overcome, you get excited and begin to summon tremendous amounts of energy. You feel like you need to prove to yourself and to others that you have the ability and the power to achieve whatever you desire.

You set goals for yourself and then determinedly work to achieve those goals because you have the confidence and self-assurance that you can do whatever you attempt. Your mission in life is to achieve all that you can in everything you do and to reap the rewards associated with this success. When you are on a mission, no one or no thing can distract you. To achieve what you desire, you will display great courage, foresight, creativity, and inspiration. You are especially motivated to do something when you are told that you can't do it—you enjoy proving people wrong about your desires and your ability to achieve.

For you, winning is everything and tends to be the strongest aspect of your spirituality. You tend to see all things in life as a game to win or lose, and you judge yourself as either the winner or loser of each contest—you don't like to lose or be outdone. In these games, you really like to win as much as possible, and rate your self-esteem based on your win–loss record. In fact, you're not even content with just winning—you have a sincere desire to dominate others and end up on top of whatever ventures you undertake. You want to be in front with everyone else following your lead, which is a function of your desire to be in control at all times. Once an idea gets in your head about the way things should be, you are not satisfied until you make it happen. If you are not in control of a situation, you often find yourself fighting for control from those in power.

You also love being right and will promote your ideas, argue to prove that your ideas are the correct ones, and, if necessary, fight to persuade others to believe in you and your ideas. However, you need to resist this instinct at times because insisting on being right every time might make you look like a dictator who is too demanding when dealing with other people.

CAESAR

Caesar is a typical Jaguar Spirituality Type who thrives on challenges and is interested in conquering other companies and businesses. He owns his own business and loves his work as a takeover specialist, or "corporate raider," taking great enjoyment in buying up smaller competitors, breaking them up, and selling off the pieces. Caesar works very hard and enjoys the rewards he receives because of his mercenary abilities. For him, every takeover is a battle that he intends to win, which he does most of the time. While the personal rewards are strong motivators, he also sees buying and "blowing up" old, nonproductive businesses as a service to people. Caesar gets very excited when a new business opportunity presents itself. In his words, it is the battle that is so exciting, not the end result. Caesar gets a spiritual high from competing with others in the business world. For him, winning tends to be everything, and every battle on his scorecard is either a win or a loss. When going after a company to buy, he sees it as an opportunity to dominate not only a competing business, but also the people who work in that business. He wants to be in charge and be the leader in everything he does. For Caesar, there is no second best; he always has to end up on top.

You seem to love the rush that accompanies confrontation. You enjoy being engaged against others on the field of battle and using your energy to thwart the obstacles that enemies place in front of you. This love of competition allows you to show yourself and others that you are the best. Thus, you are not afraid to compete with anyone about anything. This love of competition allows you to also access qualities that you never thought you had. Because it comes so naturally, sometimes you don't even realize you are competing against other people.

Finding Your Primary Influencers for Jaguar

Look back at the assessments that you completed in the introduction. The Jaguar Spirituality Type has four primary Influencers: Death, Ancestors, Wind, and Rabbit. On the chart that follows, write the scores for each of the four Influencers on the line next to that name. The highest score is the greatest influence in your life. You should then make note of how that Influencer is affecting your current Spirituality Type.

Death = _____

Rabbit = _____   JAGUAR   Ancestors = _____

Wind = _____

DEATH

Death spirituality traits influence you to harness your passion and make contributions through creative expression, writing in particular. You will feel fulfilled, content, and one with the universe when you are creating things and are driven to express your creativity. Whatever artistic projects you get involved with, you are passionate and tend to excel in activities such as entertaining, writing, drawing, painting, designing, and cartooning. If Death is Caesar's primary Influencer, he might write a textbook that colleges and universities could use in their business classes. Death influences you by tempering your interest in vanquishing others in the business world by bringing out your creative side. You will probably use your creative talents to enhance your ability to buy other businesses. For you, creating new business opportunities out of old businesses is your gift. You may even enjoy some type of creative activities in your spare time.

What creative abilities do you possess? How can you use these creative abilities in the business world?

_____

_____

_____

WIND

Wind spirituality traits influence you to be a natural-born leader. You are driven to be first and the best at whatever you do. With a natural urge to be in the trenches, you are most confident and self-assured when you are leading other people. Because you feel that your way is the best way and that others should follow your lead, you tend to rely solely on yourself to get things done. Very often, you have difficulty delegating tasks to others around you. You like breaking new ground and blazing new trails. If Wind is Caesar's primary Influencer, he might try his business techniques in a different country. Wind influences you to spend a great deal of time with the people whom you manage, as well as try new and different ways of applying your business skills. It will help you to think about new ways of building and maintaining your business, even if it means starting a different kind of business or doing business in a very different way.

What new trails would you like to blaze in your business ventures?

_____

_____

_____

RABBIT

Rabbit spirituality traits influence you to use your business skills to help green the Earth. You feel at home in the great outdoors, which is where you can best use your business and leadership skills. When you find yourself in the great, vast, green expanse of nature, your awareness expands, you feel alive, and you feel more spiritual than you can in the city. Thus, you are drawn to activities that involve being outdoors, whether you are engaged in working as a park ranger or enjoying outdoor activities like fishing or watching sporting events. Only when you are outside do you feel excited and refreshed. If Rabbit is Caesar's primary Influencer, he might buy a "green" environmental company that could help preserve the Earth's natural resources. Whether for your business or in your hobbies, Rabbit influences you to take an interest in spending time outdoors in nature, so many will start businesses that involve working outside or helping to protect the planet. Others choose to take on activities that will help preserve nature, such as recycling, cleaning up the rivers, or planting trees.

How can your business be more ecologically friendly and "green"?

_____

_____

_____

ANCESTORS

Ancestors spirituality traits influence you to use your ability to dream and use your imagination to visualize opportunities for yourself and others. Ancestors pushes you to imagine things that ordinary people cannot even imagine. You believe that if you can see something, then you can create it or make it possible. If Ancestors is Caesar's primary Influencer, upon taking over a company, he might envision a more effective way of saving (or reinstating) some of the jobs that the previous management had scaled back or eliminted. Ancestors influences you to be a dreamer, forcing you to use your imagination to dream up what others may think is impossible. Ancestor-influenced people will be amazed at the different types of solutions they can come up with for life's problems. Allow yourself time to meditate and "dream."

What types of opportunities do you visualize for your business?

_____

_____

_____

Eagle Description

You tend to love control and power. For you power and control are two sides of the same coin. The more power you can get, the more control you can get, which then makes you feel even more powerful and more in control. While you are driven to make an impact on what matters most to you in life and power allows you to do this, you understand power and the impact that it can have on your life and the lives of others. That's why in addition to being naturally attracted to other people, jobs, and recreational activities that can help you gain more power, you also have a talent for bringing out the power that other people have in them.

There are many types of power that you strive to achieve in your life and in your career, which you tend to go after efficiently and relentlessly. You like to direct the actions of others, so you are always on the lookout for social power. Because you know a lot about human psychology, you are attuned to what motivates other people. This is important information for you to acquire in your efforts to get people to go along with your plans, even though you are influential with others and enjoy managing and supervising their efforts. The ability to see very clearly what other people are capable of and then effectively bring these qualities to the forefront is a valuable skill for you.

Attaining as much status and political power as possible is an extension of social power. You love the immense influence that political power brings because it can help you make changes on a large, sometimes national or international, scale. You enjoy working with, and are very comfortable in handling, large amounts of people and resources. Competing for this type of power keeps you alert and on your toes.

Of course, you love the financial power that money can bring you—for security as well as for power. Because you know how much power money can yield, you want to possess and control as much as possible. You are not shy about putting to good use your or other people's money and other resources, because, with the right amount of money, you know you can make things happen in this world. You are also interested in reading about, studying, and investing money.

While you tend to seek power and control so that you will feel safe and secure, knowing that you can get others to do things for you is another perk of power that you enjoy. As long as you are in control, there's much less chance that something will take you by surprise. You have a certain allure that often allows you to manipulate others and get what you want. However, it works best when you attempt to channel your assertive energies into creative or altruistic activities and occupations.

You love a challenge and enjoy doing battle with other people and things, but are seldom satisfied unless you win. You thrive on competition and are quick to assert your dominance, always attempting to assert yourself as the leader in any situation, willingly fighting anyone or anything to establish your dominance. Often charging full-speed ahead, you meet challenges head-on. With a desire to be the best at what you do, you are able to clearly define and systematically set out to acquire what you want while remaining resourceful and adaptable if unexpected obstacles develop. You are very dynamic and driven to initiate new projects and take on new challenges. When you initiate a project, you do so with enthusiasm, power, intensity, and full commitment. This is how you feel excitement in your life. Your competitive spirit, resilience, confidence, and determination make achieving great things possible for you. You are direct and pull no punches. You "tell it like it is!" and can be confrontational with others when you need to.

Driven to assert yourself and get what you want in life, you also tend to be very impatient in these attempts to fulfill your needs. You have an enduring, passionate approach in the pursuit of what you want. You are quick to achieve what you want in life. You move, think, and act quickly in all you do. The boundless energy you possess often gets expressed in the role of a dominant leader. You rarely let any types of obstacles—people or things—stand in your way. This aggressiveness is what makes you an excellent leader. Honest and direct in your behavior and in speaking to others, you do not try to manipulate others. You have a fiery temper, express your rage, and then forget about the situation and the people involved just as quickly. Most times you are able to harness this anger to fuel your actions.

You are extremely self-determined in all you do. This trait provides you with a focused, reality-based, win-at-all-costs attitude that allows you to set your sights on what you want and to go and get it. Your self-determination fuels your intensity and drive. Fearless in your approach to life, you will say things and attempt to do things that most other people would not attempt. You do not let your fears hold you back. Actually, you will try to use your fears as motivating forces in your life. You are very self-reliant. You rarely listen to other's advice and feel that you can accomplish your goals by yourself. Rather than listen to what others say, you always want to try things out for yourself. Then, you rarely worry about the outcome. If you do not succeed, you will simply try again!

You are resilient in the face of challenges. Instead of worrying about various challenges, you actually thrive on them. Failing to achieve a goal or meet a challenge just makes you want to try again even more! For you, this is actually what makes life fun. You are optimistic and always believe that better things are on the horizon. Thus, you are always looking for the next project to work on. You refuse to adopt a victim mentality. Instead, you focus on the opportunities that life presents. Therefore, you are able to bounce back much faster than most in tough times. For you, hope and enthusiasm get you going on to the next mission in your life.

Because you tend to be more interested in helping yourself than in helping others, you are vulnerable to becoming too ego-driven, selfish, and self-involved. When this happens, you often forget about the needs of others and focus too much on your own. You can actually become addicted to the power that propels you to achieve so many things.

You are motivated to achieve success and be productive. You are enterprising and enjoy the rewards of your success. Ambitious and determined, you are able to set goals for yourself and then work to achieve those goals—for yourself and your employers. You have leadership capabilities and enjoy positions that require a great deal of responsibility. However, you may tend to have a rigid and stubborn spirituality.

SUSIE

Susie is a typical Eagle Spirituality Type. She is addicted to power and believes that the more power you have, the more control you have over others and the way things are done. Driven to make her town a better place to live, she loves to work on behalf of others and have others work under her leadership. A keen understanding of people and what motivates them is what makes her so good at her job. As a local politician in a small town in North Carolina, Susie feels that her ability to bring out the best in other people is what makes her successful. She loves working on behalf of her constituency and believes that political power allows her to bring about positive changes in her town, and maybe someday in the entire state. Very competitive by nature, she loves a good battle—she especially loves debating political issues with others in political power. She can very easily and very quickly assert herself, and others usually know when she means business. Like most public figures, Susie also loves the status and political power that she receives from doing her job, including being recognized in her town as sort of a celebrity there. That said, she really feels like she is improving her town for her family, as well as constituents, to live and flourish. Her job provides her with a feeling of safety and security. Servant leadership is Susie's spiritual calling.

Finding Your Primary Influencers for Eagle

Look back at the assessments that you completed in the introduction. The Eagle Spirituality Type has four primary Influencers: Deer, Night, Water, and Crocodile. On the chart that follows, write the scores for each of the four Influencers on the line next to that name. The highest score is the greatest influence in your life. You should then make note of how that Influencer is affecting your current Spirituality Type.

Deer = _____

Water = _____   EAGLE   Crocodile = _____

Night = _____

Deer

Deer spirituality traits influence you to be strong and resilient in your social advocacy and be quite forceful and direct. Your tendency to dominate most situations is why you can become a civic leader. Whether for worldly or spiritual purposes, you come on very strong with a great deal of power. You make a great leader because you have vision, trust in yourself, trust in your knowledge, and the ability to get things done. If Deer is Susie's primary Influencer, she might consider running for the senate so that she could represent her entire state, not just her town. Deer influences you to seek the most power you can possibly achieve and increases your desire to speak up on behalf of other people. You probably love the power that is associated with high-profile occupations. Many Deer-influenced people seek leisure activities that will enhance their power and standing in the community. To persuade even more people to your point of view, you may want to enhance your public speaking skills.

How can you best use this strength and resiliency to build your business?

_____

_____

_____

Night

Night spirituality traits influence you to be a very gifted speaker and communicator. With an innate need to write and express yourself, you are exceptional at using words to inspire, motivate, persuade, and entertain other people. You sincerely believe and truly understand that the pen, and the spoken word, is mightier than the sword. If Night is Susie's primary Influencer, she would use her communication and public speaking skills to further her interest in becoming a senator in her state. Night influences you to communicate your interests, passions, and vision to other people. Because you are a great communicator and motivator of other people, you are successful in the business world. Starting your own business is a distinct possibility; you will be very successful in recruiting and training people to help you achieve your vision.

How can you best use speech and written communication to enhance your business?

_____

_____

_____

Water

Water spirituality traits influence you to love to be challenged intellectually. You live to explore business ideas at work, test your hypotheses and those of others, and develop theories based on what you have read and how you have interpreted what you have read. In fact, you love to explore all new areas of information and play with developing theories to test the information—anything that can expand your mind's awareness and consciousness. You simply love learning about new and different things. If Water is Susie's primary Influencer, she might envision and develop a theory about a better way for her town to promote itself to tourists. Water influences you to love the mental challenges, thus you tend to live in your mind a lot of the time. Testing hypotheses and theories about the work you do and the ways that you could improve the business in which you find yourself is an enjoyable, ongoing process. For you, learning never stops—you truly believe in the concept of lifelong learning—and that is what keeps you ahead of your competition.

How can your love of ideas enhance your business?

_____

_____

_____

CROCODILE

Crocodile spirituality traits influence you toward the mysterious side of life and an interest in the more esoteric aspects of human nature and human development. You thrive on exploring the mysteries or hidden aspects of those things or people in which you are interested. In reality, you are a problem-solver in that you enjoy using your penetrating intelligence to discover things that you feel could be working more effectively and then using your strategic skills to improve the situation. If Crocodile is Susie's primary Influencer, she might read books about some of the organizational techniques that great leaders have used throughout history. Crocodile influences you by making human nature a puzzle to be solved. You tend to think in terms of how you can make things better for other people, often based on esoteric tools and techniques from long gone cultures. You believe that if you can discover better ways for people to work and live, you will be more successful.

How can your interest in, and knowledge of, human nature help your business practices?

_____

_____

_____

Deer Description

You make a great leader because you have vision, trust in yourself, trust in your knowledge, and the ability to get things done. You are able to follow your own creative visions and have confidence that you can sell your ideas to others and motivate them to help you carry out your ideas.

A loyal, beloved leader of other people, you motivate people and inspire loyalty by recognizing their gifts and then by bringing out the best in them. Because you are a benevolent leader, you know the value of praising the work of others, encouraging them, and making sure they know how much you appreciate their contributions. You emanate self-respect by the way you carry yourself, which, in turn, commands the respect of others around you. Your popular leadership style motivates others to envision your dreams and then to carry out the necessary steps needed to fulfill these dreams.

You enjoy attention and recognition and will do what is required to achieve it. You want others to admire and respect you. More than monetary rewards, you like compliments and having your accomplishments acknowledged. Because you know how much you enjoy flattery, you tend to give it freely to others around you.

You possess a type of visionary intuition, but are able to balance it with common sense. Understanding what needs to be done and then taking the proper steps to accomplish your goals is your practical side coming through. Although you have the ability to dream big dreams, you are quite realistic about what you can commit to, and tend to take calculated risks on things you know you can accomplish. You have this innate sense of both your interests and your abilities.

You are generally as good at what you do as you think and say you are. You are too proud to fail at anything you attempt, which is primarily why you are not afraid to take on large projects and convince others to join you. The ability to quickly come up with very clever ideas, organize a plan for implementing the ideas, and then put the plan into motion makes it easy getting others to dedicate themselves to your cause. (Your charisma and charm doesn't hurt either!) You have a rare combination for coming up with great ideas and then following through to make sure your ideas are implemented.

You are willing to do anything to achieve the goals that you set for yourself. Action-oriented, innovative, and persistent—but with very little patience—you have a strong desire to be a winner, which creates a great deal of stress and can lead to having trouble relaxing. Self-motivated and goal-oriented, you will stick with a task until it is accomplished, working at all costs to meet your set goals.

You usually take yourself very seriously and are confident in yourself, but do not feel the need to brag. However, you often have trouble getting to know people well. You should watch not to crave power and attempt to control other people, however. When this does happen, you will surely lose some of the loyalty of those people around you. Along the same lines, with your direct approach and tendency to tell it like it is, you don't worry about details or about offending other people. Others respect you because of your ability to accomplish tasks rather than the way you treat people. You need to watch that your forcefulness does not alienate other people.

Strong and self-reliant, individualistic and independent, you work hard and know how to get things done. You speak and act assertively and like to take charge and meet challenges head-on, courageously sticking up for yourself and for others. As an excellent problem-solver who often takes the initiative and enjoys being in charge of projects and others, you could savor being self-employed.

Finding Your Primary Influencers for Deer

Look back at the assessments that you completed in the introduction. The Deer Spirituality Type has four primary Influencers: Storm, Eagle, Crocodile, and Corn. On the chart that follows, write the scores for each of the four Influencers on the line next to that name. The highest score is the greatest influence in your life. You should then make note of how that Influencer is affecting your current Spirituality Type.

Julia

Julia is a typical Deer Spirituality Type. She is a true visionary in the business world. As the dean of the college of education at a small college in the northeast, she always takes the time to encourage people, compliment people when she can, and praise people for their good work. Her employees view her as an ideal, beloved leader of people. No matter what she proposes, Julia has a way of getting people to buy into her vision and then work to implement it. She takes great pride in her ability to lead others. To enhance her ability, she has taken additional leadership courses. Julia tends to be very intuitive when it comes to co-workers and employees, always seeming to know when someone needs to talk or is not feeling well. In addition, she becomes very protective if the people working for her are threatened, and she will adamantly defend them. While she likes being in the spotlight, what really drives Julia is recognition from her supervisors for the work she has accomplished. She is very confident in her abilities and will not back down from a conflict. She is very direct and assertive and is not afraid to tell her colleagues how she feels. A very persistent person, she will work to complete a project until it is finished—even when other members of her team give up. No wonder that the people working for Julia love her and appreciate her management style! She is a "take charge and get the job done" kind of person. Julia is interested in making sure that the college of education grows and improves, but not at the expense of the faculty and staff who work for her. She is intuitively visionary and is able to see the big picture and get people to help her complete this picture. Julia's supervisors appreciate her individualism, independence, and take-charge attitude.

Storm = _____

Crocodile = _____   DEER   Corn = _____

Eagle = _____

STORM

Storm spirituality traits influence you to capitalize on your intense compassion and energy to fight battles for higher causes. Your compassion and sensitive temperament allows you to better serve the world. Because of your dedication to higher goals, you are able to do naturally whatever needs to be done in order to bring people and things in society together in peace and harmony. If Storm is Julie's primary Influencer, she might travel to Third World countries and use her education and management skills to help people without schools to build and organize them. Storm influences you to become very empathetic toward the people with whom you work. You tend to hate conflict and confrontation, and always work to find peaceful solutions to life's problems. Regardless of the personal cost, you are dedicated to helping others.

How would you describe your passion and energy? How has it helped you to succeed in business?

_____

_____

_____

EAGLE

Eagle spirituality traits influence you to love control and power. For you, power and control are two sides of the same coin. The more power you can get, the more control you can get, which then makes you feel even more powerful and more in control. You are driven to make an impact on what matters most to you in life and power allows you to do this. You are naturally attracted to other people, jobs, and recreational activities that can help you gain more power. If Eagle is Julie's primary Influencer, she might work to become vice president for Academic Services, where she could use her skills for people working in all of the academic colleges, not just her own. Eagle influences you to seek all the power you can achieve, hopefully to do good deeds. You probably feel that the best way to make an impact in the lives of people is to work hard and achieve a high ranking in an organization where you can influence the lives and careers of others.

Why is power so vital to you?

_____

_____

_____

CROCODILE

Crocodile spirituality traits influence you toward the mysterious side of life and an interest in the more esoteric aspects of human nature and human development. You thrive on exploring the mysteries or hidden aspects of those things or people in which you are interested. In reality, you are a problem-solver who enjoys using your penetrating intelligence to discover things that you feel could be working more effectively and then using your strategic skills to improve the situation. If Crocodile is Julia's primary Influencer, she might explore better, more effective ways to provide services to the students in her college. Crocodile influences you by making human nature such a puzzle to be solved. You tend to think in terms of how you can make things better for other people, often based on esoteric tools and techniques from long-ago cultures. You believe that if you can discover better ways for people to work and live, you will be more successful.

How can your interest in, and knowledge of, human nature help your business practices?

_____

_____

_____

Corn

Corn spirituality traits influence you to fight for peace and justice in your community. It pulls you to be very active in social organizations and in social leadership, very often becoming a leader in community. You either have many children in your family or you play a parental role for your extended families or the people in your community. In general, you are down-to-earth, practical, and nurturing to other people. If Corn is Julia's primary Influencer, she might look for ways to include members of community groups in her curriculum. Corn influences you to be extremely nurturing in your job and your leisure activities. You are a supporter of other people and feel it's your duty to make things better for future generations. You take great pride in your interest in, and ability for, helping people to grow psychologically, spiritually, and emotionally.

How does this interest in the community affect your business practices?

_____

_____

_____

Wind Description

You tend to be a natural-born leader who is driven to be first and the best at whatever you do. You have a natural urge to be in the trenches and lead the way for others. In fact, you are most confident and self-assured when leading other people. Because you feel that your way is the best way and that others should follow your lead, you tend to rely solely on yourself to get things done, and often have difficulty in delegating tasks to others around you.

In whatever career you choose, you want to be calling the shots. You lead by what you think is right and best for everyone involved. In doing so, you make decisions quickly and decisively whether others like it or not. Your personal style is to make decisions, give people their tasks to complete, and expect them to carry your orders out as you requested.

You have a unique combination of power and a big heart—notably marked by your intense sense of loyalty and protection of others, especially those who work for you—which lends itself well to a variety of leadership positions. Everything you do and say embodies pride and honor. You have natural courage and pride that allows you to take more creative risks than other people. Your desire is to create something lasting and worthwhile for future generations. You have an air of calm self-confidence that suggests to other people that you know that you will accomplish great things in this life. When your pride gets hurt, you tend to retreat and "lick your wounds." You often put too much pressure on yourself to accomplish things.

You like breaking new ground and blazing new trails, willing to try things even if many people before you have failed. Even though you often do not know how you will achieve your goals, you just set out with the confidence that you will capitalize on opportunities as they appear and that you will ultimately be successful. A strong belief that your leadership qualities and natural abilities can make anything happen helps you plow through all obstacles until you succeed on your terms.

You are endowed with a tremendous amount of energy. Because of this you are driven to make things happen the way you want them to. This energy also drives you to discover and accomplish things that have never been accomplished before. Your vast amounts of energy provide you with the courage and relentlessness you need in pursuing your vision.

When you are blazing new trails and attempting to accomplish new and exciting things, you can be extremely motivated. You only start to worry if you have finished your projects and there are no other tasks to accomplish in the immediate future, which is why you are constantly attempting new things and creating new projects to work on. You need to have room for growth and the opportunity to lead others in blazing new trails and conquering new universes—or to set new standards for what has been done in the past. In this way, you are a true innovator and always strive to set the standard for others to follow.

You love, seek, and exude power—and have courage and charisma that helps you lead others effectively. Using your power to promote yourself and your creative vision to express yourself, you will do whatever it takes to make sure you come out on top. In addition to quickly coming up with creative ideas, you also have the social skills and the organizational skills to see your ideas through to fruition. These skills include being a master at selling your ideas and creative visions.

Others might perceive your confidence and determination as arrogance. In reality, however, you just desire to be the best at what you do. Often becoming driven by the belief that there is nothing you cannot accomplish, you are able to combine your strong will and charisma to create a dynamic force to be reckoned with. Your true power, however, comes from your ability to let your heart guide you. Your concern and love for others is one of the reasons that others will follow you easily. Given all of this, you are able to remain humble about your spirituality and your abilities.

You are highly inspired and motivated in your work and your recreational activities. However, the motivation is primarily directed toward expressing your creativity. Many things can trigger your great imagination, and your fierce energy gives you a tremendous amount of confidence in your endeavors, which allows you to take great risks to complete the projects you begin. The more a project excites you, the more risks you are willing to take. With any project that you begin, you go full-steam ahead and devote yourself 100 percent to your work. You will expend a great amount of energy in the pursuit of your passions. To accomplish your goals you will overcome any obstacles that confront you. You cannot be stopped once you set goals for yourself.

In whatever types of relationships or activities you become involved, you are driven to become fully and energetically engaged, harnessing great amounts of power to achieve whatever you desire. Your energy, which is primarily displayed through your powerful use of creative will, is your most powerful characteristic. The secret to your success is to harness your creative and intuitive gifts to stick to projects until their completion. You are determined and committed to your interests and passions. Problems arise when you become so intent on completing a project that you get stuck and are unable, and unwilling, to move on.

You are able to make things happen through your power, vitality, expression, and individuality. Sometimes, however, you feel like you should always be the center of attention.

You are extremely courageous in finding ways to express your creativity. Your heart and spirit are enormous. Because you never want to be ordinary, you are willing to take risks to achieve the success and happiness that you feel you deserve. You both strive to achieve success and enjoy being noticed for your success. To succeed, you will not let anyone or anything stand in your way. You are persistent and tend not to do anything halfway. You will jump in with both feet and begin rallying people to get behind your ideas and your vision. You are able to make projects exciting and fun, with never a dull moment.

You are strong-willed and willing to stand up for your ideas and your convictions, and will risk criticism and negativity to win people over. You tend to be a doer, willing to move forward without wasting a lot of time thinking, evaluating, and asking for others' opinions. Knowing what you want and having the confidence that you can succeed and achieve your goals, you always give the best of yourself—it's a 110 percent effort.

You make the most out of the opportunities presented in your life—even creating opportunities where none seem to exist! Possessing a certain inner as well as outer strength in your approach to life helps you to achieve what you want and to implement your vision. You also seem to be able to use this strength when times get tough and when people working for you need a lift. With a certain quiet dignity, you have a presence that cannot be denied. This presence becomes obvious when you enter a room and people see your stylish demeanor.

Sharon

Sharon is a typical Wind Spirituality Type—a natural-born leader who is driven to be first and the best at whatever she does. The manager of a chain of supply stores, she has a natural way of leading other people. Because she is so confident in making decisions and developing plans for growth, people just naturally follow her lead. However, she is a perfectionist and does not like to delegate work to others because she thinks they cannot do the work as well as she can. Sharon is a true trailblazer in the workplace who capitalizes on opportunities that most people do not even see. Sharon enjoys trying new ways of doing things in hope that her new initiatives will increase sales in the supply store business. Blessed with tremendous vision about how things ought to work, she works to make sure that her employees buy into this vision. Her employees say that she is a great leader, but does so while at the same time being cognizant of their needs. She is extremely loyal to her present employer and would not consider jumping to a new job unless her supervisor stops rewarding her accomplishments. Sharon is very motivated in whatever she decides to do and is very competitive both at work and at play. The amount of energy that she has available for whatever activity she is involved in is one of her best attributes.

Finding Your Primary Influencers for Wind

Look back at the assessments that you completed in the introduction. The Wind Spirituality Type has four primary Influencers: Jaguar, Dog, Vulture, and Rabbit. On the chart that follows, write the scores for each of the four Influencers on the line next to that name. The highest score is the greatest influence in your life. You should then make note of how that Influencer is affecting your current Spirituality Type.

Jaguar = _____

Vulture = _____   WIND   Rabbit = _____

Dog = _____

JAGUAR

Jaguar spirituality traits influence you to be interested in attempting to vanquish and conquer anything and everyone that challenges you and stands in your way. Jaguar drives you to battle with people—your primary motivation. You get excited and begin to summon tremendous amounts of energy when presented with problems to solve and obstacles to overcome. You feel like you need to prove to yourself and to others that you have the ability and the power to achieve whatever you desire. If Jaguar is Sharon's primary Influencer, she will probably work to make her company the best in the market. Jaguar influences you to keep going until you and your business have become the best they can be. You will work very hard, use great amounts of energy, and will not stop until to you achieve what you want. You will stop at nothing and step over anyone or anything that gets in your way. It is probably best that you find leisure-time activities that are not related to business so that you can effectively recharge your batteries for more business battles.

List your long- and short-range goals:

_____

_____

_____

Dog

Dog spirituality traits influence you to seek out the excitement associated with exploring and charting unknown territories. Dog pushes you to do new and exciting things and search to do things that no one has done before. You seek adventures that will test both your mental faculties as well as your physical attributes. If Dog is Sharon's primary Influencer, she might try to start her own business to compete with the one she currently works for. Dog influences you to try new things and challenge your sense of who you truly are—to "think outside of the box" and to move beyond your comfort zone. By pushing the boundaries, you can discover mental, physical, social, and spiritual attributes and levels of energy that you never thought you possessed.

What unknown territories would you like to explore? How can you use adventure to enhance your business?

_____

_____

_____

Vulture

Vulture spirituality traits influence you to be a free spirit that cannot be bound. You feel a natural affinity to be free to do whatever you want whenever you want to do it—as if your life mission is to be free to engage in as many activities and interests as possible. You are tremendously spontaneous and willing to try almost anything new. You want an exciting life, and through adventure you feel like you can stay young. If Vulture is Sharon's primary Influencer, she may want to help the chain of supply stores she works for become an international business to see if she can have the same success in another country. Vulture encourages you to seek variety in all you do. For many employees, this new adventure often leads to business opportunities in other countries. Trying to match the success you are having can be challenging.

How has being a free spirit helped in your personal and professional lives?

_____

_____

_____

RABBIT

Rabbit spirituality traits influence you to use your business skills to green the earth. You can use your business and leadership skills in the great outdoors where you feel at home, rather than being stuck in an office. When you find yourself in the great, vast, green expanse of nature, your awareness expands, you feel alive, and you feel more spiritual than you can in the city. Thus, you are drawn to activities that involve being outdoors, whether you are engaged in working as a park ranger or enjoying outdoor activities like fishing or watching sporting events. If Rabbit is Sharon's primary Influencer, she might find a way to donate part of her company's profits to environmental projects in her community. Rabbit influences you to take an interest in nature and do everything you can to protect it and spend time in it. If Sharon was unable to accomplish this at work, she may need to find hobbies that would allow her to become a greater part of nature.

How can your business be more ecologically friendly and "green"?

_____

_____

_____

Business-oriented people feel that it is their spiritual calling to be successful in the business world. If you are one of these Spirituality Types, how will you find a way to make your mark in business and industry? Think about it and write several things you would do to make your mark:

_____

_____

_____

_____

_____

_____

_____

_____

_____

_____

_____

_____

_____

_____

_____

_____

_____

_____

_____

Imaginative
Personal Energy Pattern
& Spirituality Types

The Mayan calendar encourages us to see that everything that exists is an expression of a profound and orderly intelligence; everywhere there are traces of a great mind that does everything with a purpose.

Barbara Hand Clow in *The Mayan Code*

If you have the Imaginative Personal Energy Pattern, you have an intense need to express yourself through a variety of creative endeavors. Creative expression is the medium through which you express your greatest passion in life. You express your creativity through such venues as dance, writing, design, art, and entertaining. At one time or another you have probably tried many different types of creative jobs and recreational activities.

Behaviors That Support Spiritual Experiences	Behaviors That Hinder Spiritual Experiences
• Creative	• Disorganized
• Innovative	• Sloppy
• Flexible	• Artistic
• Visionary	• Rebellious
• Idea-oriented	• Unpredictable
• Motivated	• Irresponsible
• Curious	• Impulsive
• Adaptable	• Eccentric
• Risk taker	• Silly
• Free-spirited	• Frivolous
• Dreamer	• Superficial
• Unstructured	• Careless

Primary Characteristics of Imaginative Spirituality Types

Creative expression is how you will have Extended Spiritual Experiences. Imaginative individuals love to express themselves through a variety of mediums including art, writing, sculpting, drawing, dancing, designing, and music to name a few. You may find self-expression difficult, especially in large groups. Therefore, you tend to need time by yourself for self-expression. The following list describes characteristics of Business Spirituality Types. Check off the items that are true for you:

☐ Create change

☐ Make connections between people and ideas

☐ Work on ideas that are revolutionary

☐ Dislike structure

☐ Create and share vision

☐ Find creative solutions to problems

☐ Energized by the world around me

☐ Has bursts of energy

☐ Create new products or processes

☐ See patterns in life

☐ Find new ways of doing things

☐ Seek creative and expressive activities

☐ Are idea generators

☐ Artistic creation is spiritual for me

Occupations and Leisure Activities

Many different types of activities are well suited for people with an Imaginative Personal Energy Pattern. You live to create in both your work and in your spare time. In fact, you may desire to fuse work and leisure into one activity. The following is a list of some occupations and leisure activities that will be satisfying for you and might lead to Extended Spiritual Experiences:

OCCUPATIONS

In the list that follows place an X in the box in front of occupations that you think might bring you Extended Spiritual Experiences:

Art/Entertainment

☐ Art director

☐ Art teacher

☐ Artist

☐ Architect

☐ Cartoonist

☐ Choreographer

☐ Fashion designer

☐ Interior designer

Communication

☐ Commentator

☐ Actor/actress

☐ Announcer

☐ Journalist

☐ Editor

☐ Columnist

☐ Disk jockey

Marketing/Creating

☐ Advertising director

☐ Marketing

☐ Public relations

☐ Conference planner

☐ Event planner

☐ Publicist

FREE-TIME ACTIVITIES

In the list that follows place an X in the box in front of leisure activities that you think might bring you Extended Spiritual Experiences:

☐ Singing

☐ Painting

☐ Dancing

☐ Calligraphy

☐ Sculpting

☐ Cartooning

- ☐ Watching sports
- ☐ Writing fiction
- ☐ Attending art festivals
- ☐ Writing poetry
- ☐ Stenciling
- ☐ Scrapbooking
- ☐ Literacy volunteer
- ☐ Playing a musical instrument
- ☐ Performing magic tricks
- ☐ Attending plays
- ☐ Tole painting

Imaginative Personal Energy Pattern

The Imaginative Personal Energy Pattern is comprised of the following four Spirituality Types:

MONKEY	ANCESTORS
Able to create vivid images in your head, sees holistically, creative, explores possibilities, flair for being different, likes having fun, multitalented, colorful, sensitive, unique.	Lives in dream world, imaginative, creative vision, not interested in facts, very artistic, sees big picture, reflective, pictures how things should be done before doing them, makes life more beautiful.
DEATH	NIGHT
Creating is a spiritual act, interested in fulfilling vision, brings images to life, dramatic, fun loving, driven to express creativity, enthusiastic, tireless worker, work is like play, patient, persistent, different from other people, individualistic.	Gifted writer, receives and processes information well, words come naturally, witty, entertaining, communicative, command of language, well-rounded conversationalist, loves to read, knowledgeable, clever, plays with words.

In the next section, each Spirituality Type is described in greater detail. Make note of the strength of this Type and the Influencers for you.

Monkey Description

You typically think in terms of metaphors and analogies and are able to create vivid pictures in your mind. Maintaining a holistic perspective of life allows you to always look at the big picture, whether it is a project at work, at home, or in a recreational activity. Creating ideas and exploring the possibilities in life take up a lot of your time because your mind loves contemplating all alternatives until you can develop a creative project in which to engage.

Stemming from your flair for being different from others, which adds an exciting element to the traditional and the mundane, is your ability to devise novel applications to existing services, products, and projects. Because you are continually looking for new interests and often have difficulty staying with tasks until their completion. For you, it is the creative process and not the finished product that is so exciting. Therefore, your life is often a succession of creative projects that you work at until you get tired and bored.

You sincerely feel that your purpose in life is to make the world a better and different place through your creative endeavors. As someone who's always ready to look for fun things to do and enjoy spontaneously dealing with the things that life brings, you have an exceptional ability to perceive beauty and wonder in all things around you. Because you see yourself as a unique and gifted person, especially when it comes to art and creativity, you tend to be long on vision and short on action and completion.

You are very curious and are always receptive to change. Actually, you feel like change is the best part of your lifestyle, career, and your relationships. You are open to new and different, and often unconventional, things but often don't stay with one thing long enough to master or complete it.

With so many talents, choosing one to focus on is often difficult. You seem to have a natural affinity for music and may have a gift for singing or playing a musical instrument. You might also be adept at bringing beauty into the world and expressing your creativity through working with such things as clay, paper and pencils, or cloth. You may write poems, songs, or short stories or even find an expressive conduit in acting or entertaining. Whatever path or paths you choose to express your creativity, you will be content if you add to the beauty of the world and also receive spiritual satisfaction from the creative process.

You have creativity flowing through your veins waiting for expression. Everything you do is connected with being able to express your uniqueness and individuality through creative acts. You are somewhat driven to create things, come up with creative ideas, or find creative ways to solve problems. You seem to excel at any type of creative project you undertake.

You tend to get fully absorbed and involved in whatever you do, as an intense creative energy naturally begins to flow when you initiate a new creative project. With an ability to quickly and clearly define and envision what you want to create and often spontaneously begin the creative process, at times you can create something from nothing. You will proceed patiently and persistently until your project matches your creative vision. Creative genius cannot be rushed.

You have a unique flair that includes intense colors, creative designs and art, and other things that show your uniqueness and individuality. Never wanting to be regarded as ordinary, you want everything around you, including your home, clothes, and car to reflect your unconventional ways. Considering yourself cultured and elegant with exquisite taste, you demonstrate a certain flair that becomes obvious in everything you do, not just in your creative projects. Your creativity is reflected in every aspect of your life, including your career, your relationships, and your recreational activities.

Other people often ask you for your opinion about creative projects they undertake because of your highly developed aesthetic sense, love for beautiful things in your life, and keen sense for art and creative design. Although you tend to be shy and introverted, you are very self-assured when it comes to your creative and artistic sense. Therefore, you do not tend to stand out in a crowd, and really don't want to ever be the center of attention. However, this is not always possible, as people begin to discover your artistic and creative talents.

Talent and sensitivity are two aspects of your spirituality that seem to go hand-in-hand. You bring a sense of drama to everything you do. Along with your creativity come a variety of emotions that often can interfere with your life and the creative process in your life. Try to resist the tendency to overamplify your emotions (to prevent them from taking over your life) because you are at your best when you can channel your emotions into your artistic creations.

You see everything that happens to you and to others through the lens of an artist—a talented innovator who lives life to explore, challenge, stretch the limits of your imagination, and discover new and exciting things. Your willingness to chart previously undiscovered territories knows no bounds. You are an undeniable and unconquerable dreamer in all aspects of your life. However, you also show little self-control and patience for the unfortunate realities in life. The relentless pursuit of unconventional activities, lifestyles, and occupations has left you a bit behind the times.

You do not belong in the standard business world. You are too artistic to sit behind a desk all day at a typical eight-to-five job. You need work in which you can utilize your creative vision and insight to create new realities and implement new designs. You also do not like taking orders from other people, even a supervisor. Therefore, you often like to work alone and create through your painting, sculpting, writing, architecture or any other creative field of interest.

Finding Your Primary Influencers for Monkey

Look back at the assessments that you completed in the introduction. The Monkey Spirituality Type has four primary Influencers: Night, Storm, Serpent, and Incense. On the chart that follows, write the scores for each of the four Influencers on the line next to that name. The highest score is the greatest influence in your life. You should then make note of how that Influencer is affecting your current Spirituality Type.

DAVID

David is a typical Monkey Spirituality Type. He thinks in terms of pictures in his mind. He is extremely creative and is open to every possibility in life. As an art director for an advertising agency, his specialty is identifying novel approaches to sell his customers' products and services. For David, the process of designing art for his customers' products is the thrill—not the finished product. He often leaves the pulling together of a project to his assistant. David sees art and beauty in every project he undertakes. While his job is producing creative campaigns to sell products, he sees his purpose as making life better for other people. He is a visionary, but must have people around him to implement his vision. With a very single-minded approach, he gets totally absorbed; everyone on his advertising team can feel the intensity of his creative energy. When he begins an art project for one of the advertising agency's customers, nothing can distract him, and he will continue working until it is finished to his satisfaction. He has a flair for incorporating unique colors and patterns in his designs, and sees creating as a spiritual act in and of itself. David is somewhat introverted, but can be assertive when it comes to creative license. He is not a typical businessperson, so he might have trouble fitting into a typical corporate business setting. He has long hair and a beard and often dresses in jeans or whatever clothes he is in the mood to wear. His creative genius is such that others in the advertising agency do not care what he wears or how he looks. As long as he continues to be creative and gives the clients what they want, that is all that matters.

Night = _____

Serpent = _____   MONKEY   Incense = _____

Storm = _____

NIGHT

Night spirituality traits influence you to be a very gifted speaker and communicator. With an innate need to write and express your many ideas and stories, you are exceptional at using words to inspire, motivate, persuade, and entertain other people. You sincerely believe and truly understand that the pen (and the spoken word) is mightier than the sword. If Night is David's primary Influencer, he might try doing some of the writing on the advertising campaign to see how expressive he is. Night influences you to tell your story through a variety of creative media. You probably excel at writing and want to use your writing skills in your work. You may also see the possibility of using these communication skills in writing books or poems where you can reach a larger audience than you can in your work.

How can you best use speech and written communication to enhance your creativity?

_____

_____

_____

STORM

Storm spirituality traits influence you to capitalize on your intense compassion and energy to fight battles for higher causes. You tend to be very compassionate and your sensitive temperament allows you to better serve the world. You dedicate yourself to higher causes. You are able to do naturally whatever needs to be done to bring people and things in society together in peace and harmony. If Storm is David's primary Influencer, he might decide to begin doing advertising for a nonprofit organization of interest. Storm influences you to seek out causes that you can fight for and for which you can use your creative skills. It may influence you to use your creative skills to help others, perhaps by volunteering to create advertising for organizations in the community. You might also use your skills to teach art to underprivileged children or to children in underdeveloped countries.

What artistic projects would you like to dedicate yourself to?

_____

_____

_____

SERPENT

Serpent spirituality traits influence you to express yourself through activities in which you can tap into a more divine awareness and share those experiences with other people. You are able to transcend the matters of this Earth in many spiritual ways, including religion, mystical experiences, and the teachings of various spiritual figures. If Serpent is David's primary Influencer, he might volunteer to create advertising campaigns for religious or spiritual organizations or places of worship. Serpent influences you to get involved in a religious or spiritual way, study the religious, spiritual, and mystical readings of the great cultures throughout history, and then find a way to implement this knowledge in helping others. You may even find that missionary work is an excellent way to implement this calling with a Serpent Influencer.

How can you use transcendental experiences to be more creative?

_____

_____

_____

INCENSE

Incense spirituality traits influence you to take a very philosophical approach to life, marked by attempts to discover its deepest and darkest meanings. While most people are busy trying to find a satisfactory job, get married, and have a family, you feel like your life holds more than that. You are interested in learning about yourself and the deep truths about the meaning of existence for human beings. If Incense is David's primary Influencer, he might research and explore the symbolic nature of his artistic talents. Incense influences you to seek the meaning behind what you are doing in life, to probe the meaning of life, and determine how your creativity fits into the big picture of life. You may even believe that art and creativity are ways to learn about yourself and about others. You might consider an occupation such as art therapist, through which you could help people learn about themselves through artistic endeavors.

How can this philosophical part of you be expressed artistically?

_____

_____

_____

Ancestors Description

You do not live in the world of consciousness and reality like the rest of the people in the world. You live in your own little world of dreams and imagination, which can enliven your everyday experiences with some extra zip. Thus, through your tremendous imagination and creative vision, you can easily see the big picture of what is happening in life and the way life should be.

Your ability to dream and use your imagination allows you to see all of the possibilities in your life and in your career—to imagine things that ordinary people cannot even imagine. You sincerely believe that if you can see something then you can create it or make it possible. Not terribly interested in facts or data or in finding out how something was done in the past, you prefer to evaluate a situation, picture how it could be done or how it could be done better, and then determine what needs to be done to improve the situation or make it more beautiful.

Your tremendous imagination often translates into prolific creativity. Because of this gift, you will find yourself needing to express your visions through artistic endeavors such as sculpting, music, painting, dance, acting, or writing. Your imagination can entertain almost all possibilities since you sincerely believe that almost anything is possible.

Because you can see the big picture, you are better at planning a major project than in attending to the minute details of the project. You enjoy spending time by yourself so that you can just think, reflect, and develop your visions. This time allows you to tap into your vivid imagination to develop a creative, visionary plan for action. Then you turn the plan over to other people to carry out the details of the project, and you begin developing a new plan and the process begins all over again. You feel like you did your part in the process, which is imagining what might be possible.

Finding Your Primary Influencers for Ancestors

Look back at the assessments that you completed in the introduction. The Ancestors Spirituality Type has four primary Influencers: Road, Rabbit, Jaguar, and Death. On the chart that follows, write the scores for each of the four Influencers on the line next to that name. The highest score is the greatest influence in your life. You should then make note of how that Influencer is affecting your current Spirituality Type.

JOSHUA

Joshua is a typical Ancestors Spirituality Type. Unlike the rest of us who have to live in the world of consciousness and reality, he lives in a world of imagination and possibilities. As a photojournalist for a travel magazine, he gets to use his imagination to take photographs that show people cities in countries around the world. Through his photographs he believes he can show readers things they might never imagine. Joshua has the ability to automatically approach life with the most artistic, adventurous, and nonconformist part of his brain, and expresses his vision through the photographs he takes and has published. Unsurprisingly, as a passionate and imaginative soul who is energized at the thought of introducing new and exciting photos, he is very easily bored by repetitive tasks. Almost uninterested in traditional "left-brained" organizing details, Joshua thrives on originality and prefers variety and flexibility. From his perspective, life consists of abstract and intangible patterns that seem to come alive in his photographs. With the ability to process the big picture and his finger on the pulse of change, he can easily see future trends and will put himself at risk to show people these trends through his photography. He intuitively sees what is presented in his surroundings and is able to translate that information to his readers through the camera.

Road = _____

Jaguar = _____   ANCESTORS   Death = _____

Rabbit = _____

Road

Road spirituality traits influence you to use your tremendous love of people to help as many people as you possibly can. Highly attuned to the pain and suffering of other people, your sensitivity thus fuels your mission even further, although you live a quiet life of service to others. This service often takes the form of spiritual service, but may also be accomplished through artistic vocations, counseling, teaching, and medicine. If Road is Joshua's primary Influencer, he might try to find a way that he could use his photography skills to help people in need. Road influences you to become more attuned to the suffering of other people. You will probably have a tremendous amount of empathy for others and be able to put yourself in their shoes. Road will encourage you to use your energy to show the plight of others less fortunate than most. Think about the ways you can use your empathy and your natural talents to help others make their lives more effective.

How can you best use your art to help other people by adding joy to their lives?

_____

_____

_____

RABBIT

Rabbit spirituality traits influence you to use your business skills in the greening of the Earth. You can use your business and leadership skills in the great outdoors where you feel at home, rather than being stuck behind a desk at an office. When you find yourself in the great, vast, green expanse of nature, your awareness expands, you feel alive, and you feel more spiritual than you can in the city. Thus, you are drawn to activities that involve being outdoors, whether you are engaged in working as a park ranger or enjoying outdoor activities like fishing or watching sporting events. If Rabbit is Joshua's primary Influencer, he might think about taking photographs of nature and maybe even trying to get a book of nature-related photos published in a book. Rabbit influences you to take an interest in spending time with nature, whether it is in your business or in your hobbies. Rabbit influences you to want to spend time outdoors—this is where you are your most creative. Some people will also choose to take on activities that will help preserve nature by doing such things as recycling, cleaning up the rivers, or planting trees. Use your imagination to think of all the possibilities.

How can your acts of creativity be more ecologically friendly and "green"?

_____

_____

_____

JAGUAR

Jaguar spirituality traits influence you to be interested in attempting to vanquish and conquer anything and everyone that challenges you and stands in your way. Jaguar drives you to battle with people. This is the primary motivator in your life. You get excited and begin to summon tremendous amounts of energy when presented with problems to solve and obstacles to overcome. You feel like you need to prove to yourself and to others that you have the ability and the power to achieve whatever you desire. If Jaguar is Joshua's primary Influencer, he might think about ways that his photography of other countries could lead to having his own travel show on television. Jaguar influences you to keep going until you and your art have become the best they can be. Driven by a desire to achieve a measure of artistic fame, you will work very hard and use great amounts of energy, stopping at nothing and stepping over anyone or anything that gets in your way. It is probably best that you find leisure-time activities that can help you to achieve what you want in the creative world.

List your long- and short-range goals:

_____

_____

_____

DEATH

Death spirituality traits influence you to harness your passion and make contributions through creative expression, particularly writing. You will feel fulfilled, content, and one with the universe when you are creating things and are driven to express your creativity. Whatever artistic projects you get involved with, you are passionate and find yourself excelling in activities such as entertaining, writing, drawing, painting, designing, and cartooning. If Death is Joshua's primary Influencer, he might consider writing a travel book that includes his photographs of people in other countries. Death influences you to express the creative side of yourself, whether in your work or in your spare-time activities. You are a natural-born creator, but may also want to use your writing skills to enhance your creations. Finding the right opportunity and venue to express your creativity is the key. You should think about how writing can enhance your creative expression, whether it is through writing articles about your photographs or by writing a book about some of your adventures.

How can effective communication help you creatively?

_____

_____

_____

Night Description

You are a very gifted speaker and communicator, which gives you an outlet to express many of your ideas and your stories. This need to write and express yourself is so strong that it supersedes external rewards, even the prospect of money. As exceptional as you are at using words to inspire, motivate, persuade, and entertain people, you sincerely believe and truly understand that the pen (and the spoken word) is mightier than the sword.

Your greatest gift is your ability to receive, process, and pass on information in a written or verbal format. Words seem to come very easily and naturally to you, as if there is a ready supply of words available in your head that you are able to access. You enjoy playing with words and catchy phrases as you spin tales and write your stories.

A natural-born storyteller, you almost hypnotize your audience with your clever communication style and are often described as quite witty with your ability to turn a phrase and entertain. However, you back up your style with plenty of substance. Because you are so knowledgeable about a wide variety of topics, a broad range of people find your stories compelling and entertaining.

What makes your storytelling memorable is rooted in the dynamic source of your knowledge—other people. You enjoy conversations with others about a variety of topics and are able to speak and write very eloquently about world affairs, sports, and politics. However, communication is a two-way street for you, and you place great value on exchanging ideas—you love sharing your convictions and learning about what other people think and feel about important topics. The ability to deftly integrate into the conversation information gathered from other sources, you can easily make any conversation interesting by remembering interesting quotes you have

SHANNON

Shannon is a typical Night Spirituality Type. A very gifted speaker and communicator who enjoys expressing many of her ideas and stories, she works as a public relations specialist in a mid-sized organization. She uses her writing and speaking skills to inspire and persuade people to use her organization's various products and services. Colleagues say that Shannon is very clever and witty and is great at creating promotions for the organization, which, in part, is due to her vast knowledge, intuitive knack for finding research material to support her arguments, and the ability to adapt her message to many different audiences. Words come very easily, and her writing has a poetic tone to it, as if the words dance off of her tongue and flow freely from her pen. When she is not working, Shannon likes to hang out at bookstores to see what other people are writing. She is extroverted and enjoys meeting and developing rapport with people she has never met. This ability to meet people and make them feel comfortable is very valuable in her public relations position. For Shannon, the communication of ideas through both storytelling and writing offer her the opportunity to experience many spiritual moments.

read, summarizing television and radio shows you have watched or listened to, or reconstructing a story you heard in a previous conversation. You like being with other people and finding out as much information about others as you possibly can.

Books are another great source of information that you later can use in your communications. You also love to read. Many of your ideas and writings can be attributed to ideas that you get from reading the work of other writers. You enjoy hanging out in bookstores and tend to read voraciously—often several books at a time. You are always able to remember what you read so that you can use the information later or have some great quotes to recite in a story.

You enjoy using the many tools that are associated with communication, testing your vocabulary with puzzles and word games. You often find yourself spending an inordinate amount of time talking on the telephone, surfing the Internet for information, or learning more about the newest technological advances for communicating with others.

Your love of information, writing, and language allows you to communicate your ideas to others quickly and effortlessly. Therefore, you often find yourself educating others about certain subjects. You find that you can use your skills to make information exciting, yet simple, for others to learn. Because of your ability to spin fascinating tales, you find that other people are able to easily grasp the concepts you are communicating. You are able to break down complex ideas and explain them to others in simple, practical terms.

Finding Your Primary Influencers for Night

Look back at the assessments that you completed in the introduction. The Night Spirituality Type has four primary Influencers: Eagle, Monkey, Incense, and Water. On the chart that follows, write the scores for each of the four Influencers on the line next to that name. The highest score is the greatest influence in your life. You should then make note of how that Influencer is affecting your current Spirituality Type.

Eagle = _____

Incense = _____   NIGHT   Water = _____

Monkey = _____

EAGLE

Eagle spirituality traits influence you to love control and power. For you, power and control are two sides of the same coin. The more power you can get, the more control you can get, which then makes you feel even more powerful and more in control. You are driven to make an impact on what matters most to you in life and power allows you to do this. You are naturally attracted to other people, jobs, and recreational activities that can help you gain more power. If Eagle is Shannon's primary Influencer, she might develop a portfolio of her work so that she can begin applying to bigger organizations where she can get more recognition for her work. Eagle influences you to seek all the power you can achieve, even if it means jumping from job to job. You probably feel that the best way to make an impact in the lives of people is to work hard and achieve a high ranking in an organization where you can influence the lives and careers of other people.

How do you gain power through your art?

_____

_____

_____

MONKEY

Monkey spirituality traits influence you to think in terms of metaphors and analogies and create vivid pictures in your mind. Maintaining a holistic perspective of life allows you to always look at the big picture, whether it involves a project at work, at home, or in a recreational activity. You are able to create novel applications to existing services, products, and projects. If Monkey is Shannon's primary Influencer, she might try to develop a new public relations technique that would revolutionize the industry. Monkey influences you to use your creativity to make an impact on the lives of people and animals. Adding to your effectiveness is the ability to see the big picture and not get bogged down in the day-to-day details that cause some people to procrastinate.

How can you use your creativity to help you help other people?

INCENSE

Incense spirituality traits influence you to take a very philosophical approach to life, marked by attempts to discover its deepest and darkest meanings. While most people are busy trying to find a satisfactory job, get married, and have a family, you feel your life holds more than that. You are interested in learning about yourself and the deep truth about the meaning of existence. If Incense is Shannon's primary Influencer, she might try researching and writing a self-help book that applies what she knows about networking to life in general. Incense forces you to probe the meaning of life and how your creativity fits into the big picture of life. You may even believe that art and creativity are ways to learn about yourself and about others. You might consider an occupation such as art therapist in which you could help people learn about themselves through artistic endeavors. Teaching may also be of interest to you.

How can this philosophical part of you be expressed artistically?

WATER

Water spirituality traits influence you to love being challenged intellectually. You live to explore business ideas at work, test your hypotheses and those of others, and develop theories based on what you have read and how you have interpreted what you have read. In fact, you love to explore all new areas of information and play with developing theories to test that information—anything that can expand your mind's awareness and consciousness. You simply love learning about new and different things. If Water is Shannon's primary Influencer, she might test some new innovative ideas she has for creating promotional materials for her organization. Water influences you to love mental challenges, thus you tend to live in your mind a lot of the time. You are interested in hypotheses and theories about the work you do and ways to improve your company's business. For you, learning never stops—you truly believe in the concept of lifelong learning and that is what keeps you ahead of your competition. You may want to go back to school and learn as much as you possibly can to improve your craft.

How can your love of ideas enhance the creative process?

_____

_____

_____

Death Description

You have an intense need to express yourself through a variety of creative endeavors, as if your sole purpose in life is the expression of your vast creative abilities and vision. Your passions may include such activities as entertaining, writing, drawing, painting, designing, and cartooning. Throughout your life you will probably excel at one or more of these activities.

Creative expression, in particular writing, is a spiritual experience for you. As such, you are driven to express your creativity and doing so leaves you feeling fulfilled, content, and one with the universe. You get very enthusiastic as you begin a new creative project, through which you clearly define and develop a vision to channel your creativity. When you are able to channel these energies into your projects, nothing or no one can stop you—you are bound and determined and will work tirelessly to see your creations come to fruition. In this sense, for you, creative work is actually like

JOHN

John is a typical Death Spirituality Type who is driven to express himself through a variety of creative endeavors. He is a writer for a mid-sized newspaper and feels his sole purpose in life is expressing his vast creative abilities and vision through news stories. For him, getting a story and the process of writing it is a spiritual experience. Before beginning a new story, he spends a great deal of time thinking about creative approaches. Once John gets started on a story, nothing can dampen his enthusiasm and the creative energy he is able to channel into his writing. He is relentless once he gets going on a writing project and will let nothing stand in his way. For John, writing his stories does not even feel like work—it is more like play. He tells people that he is getting paid to play at his craft. An extremely individualistic person, John enjoys working by himself—writing is his companion. As long as he can put down his thoughts in writing, he is happy and content. He does not like taking orders from other people; instead he prefers to work alone and inform others through his creative expression. He tends to be very emotional and, at times, he shows these emotions. Most people know how John is feeling most of the time. He is not afraid to appear different than most people because he believes that he is different from the average person. His ideas and abilities will allow him to do whatever he desires.

play. You are very patient and persistent while you are in the process of expressing your creativity.

You have a flair for bringing images to life through your creations and your writing. The art you produce tends to stand out because a dynamic and strong definition of yourself ultimately comes through in your work and in your play. Uniquely individualistic and not afraid to be different, you love bright colors, lavish surroundings, and unique clothes. You have a sense for the dramatic in all you do, and tend to wear your emotions on your sleeve. However, sometimes your emotions take over your life. When this happens, unfortunately, you tend to lose some of your self-control.

You will probably express your creativity through the career you choose—apt occupations involve working with children, in education, art, counseling, or journalism. Wherever you work, however, you will utilize your flair for creative expression. In business, for example, you might excel in starting your own company and creating your own products or developing your own ideas. You have great ideas and the ability to create your own empire, and also tend to excel at the marketing and sales aspects that are critical in operating a business. Although you are creative and fun-loving, you still want to work your way to the top in an organization, for it is there that you can best utilize your creative vision and creative expression.

Finding Your Primary Influencers for Death

Look back at the assessments that you completed in the introduction. The Death Spirituality Type has four primary Influencers: Flint, Jaguar, Incense, and Road. On the chart that follows, write the scores for each of the four Influencers on the line next to that name. The highest score is the greatest influence in your life. You should then make note of how that Influencer is affecting your current Spirituality Type.

Flint = _____

Ancestors = _____   DEATH   Road = _____

Jaguar = _____

FLINT

Flint spirituality traits influence you to be a leader in the community. You believe that you represent the social standards, morals, and values of society and often feel you are the voice for other people, especially those less fortunate than yourself. Because of your interest in uncovering conspiracies and wrongdoing about a variety of social issues, you will gladly speak out about any injustices you uncover in society. You are very committed to causes you believe in. If Flint is John's primary Influencer, he might ask his editor if he could begin writing articles about social issues in his community and in the world, or ask if he could start a column that dealt with social-justice issues. Flint will influence you to take up the cause for others who have a difficult time—or are unable to—defending themselves. You are an activist at heart, whose voice must be heard, and you will use your writing skills to make your voice heard by all who will listen. You will gain tremendous satisfaction by being a civic leader, and you might even consider writing a book about volunteer activism.

What causes would you like to dedicate your artistic talents to?

_____

_____

_____

JAGUAR

Jaguar spirituality traits influence you to be interested in attempting to vanquish and conquer anything and everyone that challenges you and stands in your way. Jaguar drives you to battle with people as your primary motivation. You get excited and begin to summon tremendous amounts of energy when you are presented with problems to solve and obstacles to overcome. You feel the need to prove to yourself and to others that you have the ability and the power to achieve whatever you desire. If Jaguar is John's primary Influencer, he would want to work on a story that could ultimately win a Pulitzer Prize. Such an honor would allow him to move to a larger newspaper in a bigger city. Jaguar influences you to keep going until you and the talents you possess are recognized as the best in the business. To achieve what you want, you will work very hard, use great amounts of energy—stopping at nothing to plow through anyone or anything that gets in your way. You may even work on the story in your spare time, but be careful not to get too burned out pursuing your dream.

List your long- and short-range goals:

_____

_____

_____

Ancestors

Ancestors spirituality traits influence you to use your ability to dream and use your imagination to visualize opportunities for yourself and others. Ancestors pushes you to imagine things that ordinary people cannot even imagine. If you believe that if you can see something, then you can create it or make it possible. If Ancestors is John's primary Influencer, he might try writing a creative novel, or a book that details his exploits as a newspaper journalist. Ancestors influences you to be a dreamer—forcing you to use your imagination to dream up what others may think is impossible—but you will also work hard to achieve your dream. Ancestor-influenced people will be amazed at the different types of solutions they can come up with for life's problems. Allow yourself time to meditate and "dream."

What types of opportunities do you visualize for yourself and your art?

_____

_____

_____

ROAD

Road spirituality traits influence you to use your tremendous love of people to help as many people as you possibly can. Highly attuned to the pain and suffering of people, your sensitivity fuels your mission even further, although you live a quiet life of service to others. This service often takes the form of spiritual service, but it may also be accomplished through artistic vocations, counseling, teaching, and medicine. If Road is John's primary Influencer, he might volunteer some time helping others at a mental-health clinic or hospital. Road encourages you to become more empathetic to the suffering of others. It allows you to move beyond your ego and your success and suffering to put yourself in the shoes of others and understand what they are experiencing. Think about how you can use your empathy and your ability to help others make their lives more effective. You possess creative skills that could be very helpful in reducing the suffering of others.

How can you best serve humanity through your art?

_____

_____

_____

Imaginative-oriented people find spirituality through a variety of creative endeavors. If you are one of these Spirituality Types, how will you use your creativity to make the world more aesthetically pleasing? Think about it and write several ideas you would like to share with the world through your creativity:

_____

_____

_____

_____

_____

_____

_____

_____

_____

_____

_____

_____

_____

_____

_____

_____

_____

6

Understanding
Personal Energy Pattern
& Spirituality Types

As we get away from judging the success of our day on how much we can produce and move closer to basing our day on aligning with creation, it becomes helpful to have guidance as to where to focus our energy.

JAMES ENDREDY IN *Beyond 2012*

If you have the Understanding Personal Energy Pattern, you are bright and curious. You tend to be a student at heart. You are happiest when you are in the pursuit of knowledge and wisdom. Thus, you are eager to learn about everything you possibly can. You seek information about yourself, and you prize knowledge gained through self-discovery. You are continually searching for experiences that will lead to "Aha" knowledge. You are very inquisitive and are driven by the desire to learn new things, question life and human existence, and search for answers to the meaning of life. You have a love for thinking and knowledge.

Behaviors That Support Spiritual Experiences	Behaviors That Hinder Spiritual Experiences
• Logical	• Conservative
• Analytical	• Humorless
• Detailed	• Obsessive
• Deliberate	• Perfectionistic
• Serious	• Inflexible
• Reserved	• Narrow-minded
• Focused	• Stubborn
• Tenacious	• Distant
• Organized	• Critical
• Planning	• Arrogant
• Punctual	• Negative

Primary Characteristics of Understanding Spirituality Types

Your love and search for knowledge is what leads you to Extended Spiritual Experiences. Understanding-oriented individuals are driven by a search for knowledge and understanding. You often focus on collecting facts as you want to know why and how things happen. You are constantly analyzing and evaluating to try to find the answers you seek. The following list describes characteristics of Understanding Spirituality Types. Check off the items that are true for you:

☑ Plays with theories and models

☐ Develops a logical framework for exploring possibilities

☐ Everything is subject to critique

☑ Faith is important

☐ Abstract ideas are a good thing

☐ Wants to understand a problem in depth

☑ Seeks answers to life's existential questions

☑ Enjoys learning

- ☐ Integrates ideas from a variety of sources

- ☐ Enjoys working with abstract concepts

- ☑ Needs time alone to reflect

- ☐ Is open to new ideas

- ☐ Looking for evidence to prove or disprove ideas

- ☑ Lifelong learning is the key to life and career success

Occupations and Leisure Activities

Many different types of activities are well suited for people with an Understanding Personal Energy Pattern. You truly believe that knowledge is power and you want to gain as much knowledge about yourself and the world as you possibly can. The following is a list of some occupations and leisure activities that will be satisfying for you and might lead to Extended Spiritual Experiences:

OCCUPATIONS

In the list that follows place an X in the box in front of occupations that you think might bring you Extended Spiritual Experiences:

Religious Studies
- ☐ Clergy

- ☐ Christian missionary

- ☒ Religious scholar

- ☐ Religious leader

- ☐ Children's religious leader

Social Scientist
- ☐ Anthropologist

- ☐ Archeologist

☐ Archivist

☐ Historian

☐ Philosopher

☐ Political scientist

☐ Sociologist

☐ Survey researcher

☒ Writer

Scientific/Medical

☐ Medical researcher

☐ Medical scientist

☐ Research psychologist

☐ Museum technician

☐ Geographer

☐ Chemist

☐ Astronomer

☐ Biologist

FREE-TIME ACTIVITIES

In the list that follows, place an X in the box in front of leisure activities that you think might bring you Extended Spiritual Experiences:

☐ Astronomy

☐ Visiting science museums

☐ Rocket building

☐ Visiting planetariums

☒ Star gazing

- ☐ Collecting rocks
- ☐ Weather watching
- ☐ Organizing church groups
- ☐ Amateur archeology
- ☒ Reading
- ☐ Reading religious scholars
- ☒ Studying religious texts
- ☐ Reading early philosophers
- ☒ Taking courses in an area of interest
- ☐ Helping in a mental-health clinic

Understanding Personal Energy Pattern

The Understanding Personal Energy Pattern is comprised of the following four Spirituality Types:

INCENSE	WATER
Philosophical, interested in discovering things, seeks deeper aspects of existence, wants wisdom about the meaning of life, seeks a connection with something grander, interprets human behavior, meant to do something great in life, seeker.	Loves to be challenged intellectually, loves ideas and hypotheses, tests theories, loves learning new things, reads a lot, adopts many nontraditional notions, writes about original thoughts, thinker, hangs out in bookstores, conceptualizes easily.
CROCODILE	SERPENT
Complex spirituality, deeply emotional, analyzing mind, mysterious, private, problem-solver, transforms negatives into positives, perceptive, healer, intuitive, lets go of own ego, wants what is best for society, sensitive, gentle, understands complexities.	Lives for transcendence, wants to tap into Greater Power, religious, spiritual, believes we are all interconnected, selfless, wants to get in touch with essence or soul, forgiving, interested in a variety of spiritual figures, seeks the mystical in life.

In the next section, each Spirituality Type is described in greater detail. Make note of the strength of this Type and the Influencers for you.

Incense Description

You tend to take a very philosophical approach to life, with a notable emphasis in attempting to discover its deepest and darkest meanings. While most people are busy trying to find a satisfactory job, get married, and have a family, you feel your life holds more than that. You are interested in learning about yourself and the deep truth about the meaning of existence for human beings.

In order to be truly self-fulfilled, you will attempt to fully immerse yourself in experiences and subjects that provide you with intuitions and insights related to the greater meaning in life. You crave experiences that connect you to something more grand than the ordinary life most people live. You seek wisdom about the meaning of life, man's place in the universe, and why we are here on Earth.

Although you ultimately seek answers to the big questions, you realize that pieces of the puzzle can be found every day. You enjoy interpreting life and human behavior, and you love the insight this brings to you and to others in the world. Always seemingly able to put a positive spin on things and remain upbeat in the face of darkness and stress helps you garner information in everything as you seek to find a higher power in all you do. Your rare ability to find meaning in any type of suffering is largely accomplished by looking beyond the tiny annoyances of daily life.

Because of your Spirituality Type, you tend to always adopt a broad perspective on your life and your career. You like to focus on the meaning involved in your activities and refuse to let obstacles and setbacks bring you down. Relying on philosophies like "it's not the end of the world" or "it could have been worse" to remain upbeat and joyful, you will go out of your way to make the best of a situation and to find the best qualities in every person you meet.

You feel you were meant to do something really important in this life, which can motivate you to be the best person you can be. Because you often find meaning in the philosophical questions about life through your work or recreational activities, you are always on the lookout for your "calling" in life or what you were truly put

Samantha

Samantha is a typical Incense Spirituality Type who takes a philosophical approach to her life and her career. She teaches psychology at a community college in the midwestern United States, and she remains interested in learning all she can about life and the meaning of life. The great enjoyment she gets from interpreting life and human behavior is passed on to her students. Since she sees psychology and philosophy as her "calling" in life, she tries to help other people find their calling too. A truly introspective person who enjoys learning all she can about herself and other people, Samantha always seeks the deep truth about the meaning of human existence. Existential questions like "Why are we here?" and "How did we get here?" continually pop into her mind as she seeks wisdom about the meaning of life, our place in the universe, and why we are here on Earth. She finds herself getting so caught up in finding the meaning in life that she often forgets about her own life. While religious, Samantha describes her path as more of a spiritual journey than a human journey. Firmly believing that having fulfilling experiences is more important than accumulating "things" in life, Samantha seeks experiences that allow her to learn about herself and her makeup as a person. This entails meditating at home, getting massages, and learning how others view spirituality. Often she can be found in the library reading books about the spiritual practices of people in different religions and cultures. She often laughingly says that when she is able to find the meaning, she will be able to retire and relax a little bit.

on this Earth to do. This often leaves you on a never-ending search for meaning and fulfillment in your life, relationships, and career.

It is through acts of loving and discovering the deeper nature of your experiences that you find meaning. You often find yourself meditating to find the answers to life's existential questions. Thus, you gather wisdom in life by being a seeker, then a teacher. Very often, as you are learning about things, other people will seek you out for information or your views about the meaning of life. Since you were a child, you have always searched for greater understanding of the meaning of life. It is this search for answers that you live for.

You live your life in anticipation of coming across knowledge that will provide you with answers to the question "What is the meaning of all of this?" Therefore, you find yourself learning about new things in a variety of ways, including reading books, watching television shows, and surfing the Internet.

Finding Your Primary Influencers for Incense

Look back at the assessments that you completed in the introduction. The Incense Spirituality Type has four primary Influencers: Water, Serpent, Monkey, and Night. On the chart that follows, write the scores for each of the four Influencers on the line next to that name. The highest score is the greatest influence in your life. You should then make note of how that Influencer is affecting your current Spirituality Type.

Water = 10

Monkey = 11   INCENSE   Night = 7

Serpent = 10

WATER

Water spirituality traits influence you to enjoy being challenged intellectually. Your mind loves to work with ideas, thoughts, and hypotheses that can expand your mind's awareness and consciousness. You live to explore ideas at work, test your hypotheses and those of others, and develop theories based on what you have read and how you have interpreted what you have read. In fact, you just love exploring new areas of information and playing with developing theories to test the information. You simply love learning about new and different things. If Water is Samantha's primary Influencer, she might test and research several different hypotheses about human nature that she could eventually turn into a self-help book. Water influences you to love the mental challenges, thus you tend to live in your mind more often than most people. You are interested in researching hypotheses and theories about why people do the things they do and ways that you could improve the business in which you find yourself. For you, learning never stops—you truly believe in the concept of lifelong learning and that is what keeps you ahead of your competition. Find the best ways to become a lifelong learner.

What types of ideas and hypotheses do you like to work with?

The differences between men and women. Relationships and spiritual practice.

SERPENT

Serpent spirituality traits influence you to express yourself through activities in which you can tap into a divine awareness and share these experiences with other people. You are able to transcend the matters of this Earth in many spiritual ways, including religion, mystical experiences, and the teachings of various spiritual figures. If Serpent is Samantha's primary Influencer, she might try to identify the meaning of life by learning about and practicing information from some of the world's most popular spiritual and religious traditions. Serpent influences you to get involved in a religious or spiritual way and to study the religious, spiritual, and mystical readings of some of the great cultures throughout history, and then find a way to use this knowledge to help others. Some find that missionary work is an excellent way to implement this calling with a Serpent influencer. Serpent influences you to seek out and find ways to integrate a spiritual component to whatever work you are doing.

What types of spiritual ideas inform your intellectual journey?

_____

_____

_____

Monkey

Monkey spirituality traits influence you to think in terms of metaphors and analogies and create vivid pictures in your mind. Maintaining a holistic perspective of life allows you to always look at the big picture, whether it is a project at work, at home, or in a recreational activity. You are able to create novel applications to existing services, products, and projects. If Monkey is Samantha's primary Influencer, she might develop a website that proposes a new self-help system for people who are seeking meaning in their lives. She might look for creative ways to introduce her students to the great psychologists throughout history. Monkey influences you to use your creativity to make an impact on the lives of people and animals. Adding to your effectiveness is the ability to see the big picture and not get bogged down in the day-to-day details that cause some people to procrastinate.

How can you use your creativity to help you develop ideas and hypotheses?

By continuing to blog, write and design clothing with a message.

_____

Night

Night spirituality traits influence you to be a very gifted speaker and communicator. With an innate need to write and express yourself, you are exceptional at using words to inspire, motivate, persuade, and entertain other people. You sincerely believe and truly understand that the pen (and the spoken word) is mightier than the sword. If Night is Samantha's primary Influencer, she might consider writing a book about the meaning of life or go on a speaking tour on that same subject. Night influences you to communicate your interests, passions, and vision to other people. Because you are a great communicator and motivator of other people, you are successful in the business world. You might consider working as a private consultant or a motivational speaker. You may even want to try starting your own business; you will be very successful in recruiting and training people to help you achieve your vision.

How can you best use speech and written communication on your spiritual journey?

_____

_____

_____

Water Description

You love to be challenged intellectually. You live to explore ideas, test your hypotheses and those of others, and develop theories based on what you have read and how you have interpreted what you have read. Anything that can expand your mind's awareness interests you because you simply love learning about new and different things.

No matter what interests you at the time, you set off on a course to become an expert in that subject area. For you, the challenge lies in the lifelong learning process. Ultimately you hope to discover a breakthrough idea or develop a brand-new theory. In your mind when this happens, you not only add to the existing body of information and knowledge in a particular area, you will be forever remembered for the new idea or theory that you developed. For you, this would be the most exciting thing that could happen to you.

The learning process is not, however, a solitary pursuit. Although you love to think about, read about, and research notions that are full of mystery and wonder—and eagerly gather information about such topics as ancient religions, astronomy, psychology, the environment, foreign countries, mathematics, and philosophy to name a few. you also love being around other people who can challenge you intellectually. You seek them out and love to debate your ideas and notions with other people. However, you rarely take other people's ideas as fact, much preferring to research and test them for yourself. You also spend a lot of time observing others from a detached point of view and gathering information from any sources you have available to you.

It's your curiosity that propels you, acting as fuel for your exceptionally quick mind. Always collecting and integrating information through readings about different ideas, views, and beliefs, you often find yourself interested in adopting some of the nontraditional notions about family, life, religion, and culture. You are definitely a student of the world, and will tend to seek the truth wherever it may exist.

Even your pastimes result in collecting more information. You enjoy reading books, learning about various subjects in depth, and having stimulating conversations with a few special friends. In addition to finding yourself playing intellectually challenging games and attending lectures, you also love just hanging out in bookstores and libraries. In bookstores you may not even buy anything, you just enjoy looking at all of the knowledge and information contained there. Other recreational activities you enjoy include going to concerts, theater productions, museums, and lectures.

Despite spending a lot of time out in the world and observing it, your most comfortable mode of functioning is thinking rather than feeling or acting. With the ability to think very practically and concretely as well as the ability to conceptualize things very easily, your mind is always working, thinking, evaluating, processing, and synthesizing information. Even if you would like it to, your mind never seems to stop—it tends to jump from thought to thought and topic to topic very easily and smoothly. A creative individual possessing a vivid imagination, you are also quick to develop ideas and create possibilities for yourself and for other people. Because you are interested in learning about a wide variety of subjects, you have the ability to see both the big picture as well as the most minute facts. With this ability to adapt your thinking style, you can fit in and relate effectively to a wide variety of people and in a wide variety of situations.

You have a great memory and are often able to recall information, remember people's names, and repeat information that you heard before. However, your mind is able to do more than just memorize facts—you are also gifted with great insight. Even if you do not know how you know things, you are able to draw conclusions and have great empathy for others. Knowledge and wisdom come very quickly to you and not just from the evaluation of facts, but also from intuitive means. You often build your openness to intuitive insights by learning all you possibly can about a subject of interest to you. Your mind is able to do more than just memorize facts. By effectively organizing information, correlating it, synthesizing it, and making the information meaningful, you do not get bogged down in details but keep looking at the big picture.

Greatly interested in how the world works, you are constantly asking questions and searching for answers to your questions. However, you do not accept the opinions of others nor do you readily accept traditional, time-tested doctrines. You want to better understand life and in order to do so you develop theoretical explanations for why things happen in this world. For you, understanding life is almost as fun as living it yourself. When you feel insecure you step back into the safety of your mind and knowledge.

Although you spend a lot of time and energy observing and listening to the world and contemplating why things happen as they do, you spend a lot of your time alone. You then enjoy getting praise and confirmation for your understanding of how the world works. Valuing knowledge, insight, and understanding, you are a quiet person whose sense of self is developed because of your ability to generate theories and hypotheses about the world and about human behavior. Often drawn to the unusual, bizarre, overlooked, and unthinkable, you enjoy investigating areas and subjects that have yet to be explained. In order to attain independence and confidence, you are interested in building a unique niche for yourself. You usually become focused on becoming an expert in one area of interest and will devote a lifetime to this interest if it helps to develop your identity. Because of this intensity, it is possible for you to develop remarkable theories and create ingenious innovations.

COREY

Corey is a typical Water Spirituality Type. He loves to be challenged intellectually and his mind is constantly working. A computer programmer who loves to work with ideas, thoughts, and hypotheses, he loves programming computers to complete a variety of tasks. Corey enjoys exploring hypotheses and testing ideas by writing different types of programs, and lives to explore new areas of information and play with developing theories to test the information—computers are simply his tools for this exploration. Ultimately he wants to discover a new way of programming that will revolutionize the way people use computers. Corey is also interested in becoming known as a world expert when it comes to computer programming. That's why he loves being around, talking to, and exchanging ideas with other people who share his passion for computers. In his spare time, he reads all that he can about new breakthroughs in various aspects of technology. He is most comfortable engaged in activities in which he is using his mental faculties, rather than activities that involve feelings and relationships. His mind never stops—he is always thinking, analyzing, synthesizing, and processing information. He has a tremendous memory and is able to recall information very easily—almost like a computer. Corey is very quiet and likes to spend time by himself. His energy tends to be mental energy.

Finding Your Primary Influencers for Water

Look back at the assessments that you completed in the introduction. The Water Spirituality Type has four primary Influencers: Crocodile, Incense, Night, and Eagle. On the chart that follows, write the scores for each of the four Influencers on the line next to that name. The highest score is the greatest influence in your life. You should then make note of how that Influencer is affecting your current Spirituality Type.

Crocodile = 11

Night = 7   WATER   Eagle = 4

Incense = 10

CROCODILE

Crocodile spirituality traits influence you toward the mysterious side of life and an interest in the more esoteric aspects of human nature and human development. You thrive on exploring the mysteries or hidden aspects of those things or people that interest you. In reality, you are a problem-solver in that you enjoy using your penetrating intelligence to discover things that you feel could be working more effectively and then using your strategic skills to improve the situation. If Crocodile is Corey's primary Influencer, he might look for technological solutions to address many of the problems that older people experience when trying to use new technology. Crocodile influences you to think about human nature—in Corey's case, the nature of computer operations is a puzzle to be solved. Thinking in terms of how you can make things better for other people, often based on esoteric tools and techniques from culture long gone, you will research old theories and techniques to use as your basis for new and improved ways of doing things. You believe that if you can discover better ways for people to work and live, you will be more successful.

What types of esoteric knowledge do you enjoy reading about?

The Tarot, numerology, astrology, magic, herbology and angels.

INCENSE

Incense spirituality traits influence you to take a very philosophical approach to life, marked by attempts to discover its deepest and darkest meanings. While most people are busy trying to find a satisfactory job, get married, and have a family, you feel your life holds more than that. You are interested in learning about yourself and the deep truth about the meaning of existence for human beings. If Incense is Corey's primary Influencer, he might try and find a way to develop a computer or a robot that is intelligent and can think for itself. Incense forces you to probe the meaning of life and how your creativity fits into the big picture of life—even considering the notions that art and creativity are ways to learn about yourself and about others. You might consider an occupation such as art therapist, through which you could help people learn about themselves through artistic endeavors. You probably believe that all people are philosophers searching for the meaning of life.

How can this philosophical part of you be expressed intellectually?

NIGHT

Night spirituality traits influence you to be a very gifted speaker and communicator. With an innate need to write and then express your many ideas and stories, you are exceptional at using words to inspire, motivate, persuade, and entertain other people. You sincerely believe and truly understand that the pen and the spoken word are mightier than the sword. If Night is Corey's primary Influencer, he might develop a communications guide that would help technologically oriented people become more emotionally intelligent. Night influences you to communicate your interests, passions, and vision to other people through the written word. Because you are a great communicator and motivator of other people, you are successful in the business world. The secret for you is to identify the type of business where you can use your tremendous communication skills.

How can you best use speech and written communication to enhance your search for knowledge?

_____

_____

_____

Eagle

Eagle spirituality traits influence you to love control and power. For you, power and control are two sides of the same coin. The more power you can get, the more control you can get, which then makes you feel even more powerful and more in control. You are driven to make an impact on what matters most to you in life, and power allows you to do this. You are naturally attracted to other people, jobs, and recreational activities that can help you gain more power. If Eagle is Corey's primary Influencer, he might work to develop a new technology, based on his computer experience, that he could sell to the highest bidder, or start his own technology corporation and sell the product. Eagle influences you to seek all of the power, fame, and fortune you can achieve. You are relentless in your pursuit of power. You probably feel that the best way to make an impact in the lives of people is to work hard and achieve a high ranking in an organization where you can influence the lives and careers of other people.

How does power influence your search for the truth?

Knowledge and evolution are the ultimate power.

Serpent Description

You most often express yourself through activities in which you can display your propensity for transcendence. You are able to transcend the matters of this Earth in many spiritual ways including religion, mystical experiences, and the teachings of various spiritual figures. Because your consciousness seems to be able to expand beyond the limits of this world and attempts to tap into a more divine awareness, you seem to know certain things about human life and human existence that most people are unaware of. You truly believe that all people are somehow interconnected and are one spiritually and have probably engaged in activities in which you have had the privilege to experience a type of connecting and merging with other people.

You have a quality of selflessness in which you are able to transcend your ego, your body, and even your mind and thereby connect with an expanded sense of self—you are definitely in touch with your essence, your spirit, and your soul. Quite aware that you feel an intense love and compassion for people and want to do what you can to alleviate the suffering of all people, you often call on this compassion to help others to live more effectively on Earth.

Being a very religious person who lives life according to specific religious principles, you have a unique relationship with your higher power and spiritual figures. You believe that you, and all other people on Earth, can best live if you do so in accord with a set of spiritual beliefs. Because of your intense identification with spiritual figures, you believe that forgiveness, altruism, and sacrifice in your own life will lead to redemption. The redemptive messages signified by the teachings of a variety of spiritual figures are a constant focus for you. You enjoy religions because of their messages of hope, their rituals, and their musical devotions. You tend to devote your life to a religious path so that you can directly experience your higher

Megan

Megan is a typical Serpent Spirituality Type. A missionary who is currently working to make life better for people in Romania, she feels that helping others and sharing her spiritual beliefs with others is how she can tap into her own spiritual nature. Through her work as a missionary, she is able to transcend the problems that plague many people in our society and is able to share with others the teachings of spiritual leaders that she follows. Megan believes that all people are interconnected and that by helping others she can achieve true spirituality. Selfless in her approach to helping the people of Romania and truly loving the people with whom she works, she feels that her mission in life is to alleviate the suffering of other people and be as compassionate to other people as possible. She truly believes that all people are interconnected, regardless of their cultural or religious beliefs. She wanted to live among the people of Romania and help in a hands-on way. Because she is committed to helping others, she does not care about her own needs. Although she lives in a one-room house that was abandoned long ago, has to walk about a mile each day to get water, and has only three or four things to wear, she is happy and content as long as she is able to get in touch with her spirituality through helping the people of this country. She does not worry about getting paid or having things that most people take for granted. She is a transcendent force that feels compassion very deeply.

power. You love engaging in activities in which you will have mystical experiences that transcend all earthly structures and forms.

More concerned with spiritual matters than you are biological or material matters, your relationship with a spiritual source tends to be beyond your bodily senses, time, and the world as we know it. By devoting yourself to the development of your inner life through specific spiritual practices, you seek a connection with a reality greater than yourself, one that may include the emotional experience of religious awe, salvation, or liberation.

Finding Your Primary Influencers for Serpent

Look back at the assessments that you completed in the introduction. The Serpent Spirituality Type has four primary Influencers: Incense, Corn, Storm, and Monkey. On the chart that follows, write the scores for each of the four Influencers on the line next to that name. The highest score is the greatest influence in your life. You should then make note of how that Influencer is affecting your current Spirituality Type.

Incense = 10

Storm = 12   SERPENT   Monkey = 11

Corn = 8

INCENSE

Incense spirituality traits influence you to take a very philosophical approach to life, marked by attempts to discover its deepest and darkest meanings. While most people are busy trying to find a satisfactory job, get married, and have a family, you feel your life holds more than that. You are interested in learning about yourself and the deep truth about the meaning of existence for human beings. If Incense were Megan's primary Influencer, she might study the relationships between the great philosophers and the great religious leaders, and then apply their teachings or teach others about these writings. Incense forces you to probe the meaning of life, and you receive meaning in life from helping other people grow psychologically, socially, and spiritually. You believe that the search for the truth is the greatest search anyone can undertake. You might consider any occupation in which you are able to research and apply philosophical teachings. Teaching may also be of interest to you.

How can this philosophical part of you guide your search for meaning in life?

_____ _____

_____ _____

_____ _____

Co
Co … peace and justice in your com-
mu … anizations and in social leader-
shi … t uncommon. You either have
ma … role for your extended families
or … e down-to-earth, practical, and
nu … imary Influencer, she might de-
vel … thers to become involved in ser-
vic … e world. Corn influences you to
be … pporter of other people and feel
it's … rations. You take great pride in
you … row psychologically, spiritually,
and … n and leisure interests in which
you

Ho … ch?

_____ _____

_____ _____

STORM

Storm spirituality traits influence you to capitalize on your intense compassion and energy to fight battles for higher causes. You tend to be very compassionate and your sensitive temperament allows you to better serve the world. You are able to do naturally whatever needs to be done in order to bring people and things in society together in peace and harmony. If Storm were Megan's primary Influencer, she might choose a specific need to champion. For example, she might take up the baton for getting rid of hunger in Third World countries. Storm influences you to seek out causes that you can fight for to make the world a better place for future generations. It may prompt you to use your nurturing skills to help others, maybe by volunteering with local nonprofit organizations. You might also use your skills to teach underprivileged children or teach children in underdeveloped countries. You are a force to be reckoned with once you find the cause for which you would like to fight. Some examples of these types of causes include hunger, education for underprivileged students, war, crime, the environment, or animal abuse.

What cause or causes would you like to dedicate yourself to?

_____

_____

_____

MONKEY

Monkey spirituality traits influence you to think in terms of metaphors and analogies, and are able to create vivid pictures in your mind. Maintaining a holistic perspective of life allows you to always look at the big picture, whether it is a project at work, at home, or in a recreational activity. You are able to create novel applications for existing services, products, and projects. If Monkey were Megan's primary Influencer, she might develop a website that could inform people about the causes she is currently championing. Monkey influences you to use your creativity to make an impact on the lives of people and animals. You must find the venue through which you will implement your creative skills. Monkey influences you to see the big picture and not get bogged down in the day-to-day details that cause some people to procrastinate.

How can you use your creativity in your search for meaning?

_____

_____

_____

Crocodile Description

You have a very complex spirituality orientation. Possessing deep emotions and a probing and analyzing mind, you tend to be a very mysterious and private person, and you thrive on exploring the mysteries or hidden aspects of those things or people in which you are interested. But you are also a problem-solver in that you enjoy using your penetrating intelligence to discover things that you feel could be working more effectively and then using your strategic skills to improve the situation.

With a very perceptive mind that allows you to bring into the open and into the light those things that are hidden or unused, you specialize in transforming negatives about people or the world into something positive and effective. By doing so, you are able to heal and initiate progress where there has been none in the past.

You are powerful and constantly face challenges that require you to use this power. By properly harnessing your power, however, you are quite able to bring about positive transformations in yourself and in those around you. However, you need to be aware of this power because of your tendency to wander toward the negative side of life. At times you tend to get caught up in your own negativity, which will tend to diminish your capability to transform the ineffective people and things around you. You need to watch not to become too cynical when things are not going well for you. Creative transformation is your greatest asset.

One way that you can lift yourself out of your emotional and cognitive darkness is by using your abilities to creatively transform people and things. When able to use your intuitive thinking powers in a search for solutions to a problem, you will make the most of your situation. You are willing to let go of what your ego desires in order to do what is necessary to contribute the greatest good for society. You have a special skill for examining situations objectively and understanding the complexities of that situation. By doing so, you are able to spark your own and others' imaginations in a truly transformational way.

The emotional side of your nature tends to drive you, and you often feel things very deeply and use your emotional energy as a pathway to transformation for yourself and for those around you. As you grow older, you know what you want and how you can use your powerful emotions to get what you want. Emotional desires continue to motivate you, pushing you to take risks and actions that other people might not.

A true feeler in life, you are highly sensitive to your own and to other's feelings, as well as very sensitive to what is going on around you. It is as if you have a sixth sense that provides you with information about subtle things going on in your environment. This emotional nature, however, also makes you very vulnerable. You are gentle in how you approach life and the people and challenges you encounter. You tend to want to be liked and loved by other people and often get hurt if you are not. This vulnerability, therefore, is one of the primary reasons for your tremendous transformational power.

You want to use your tremendous emotional energy to benefit yourself and others in society. The secret to your success, however, is your ability to channel your emotional energy away from the negative aspects of life to the more positive expressions that can heal, revitalize, and actualize. Throughout your life you have probably experienced the full gamut of possible emotions. Your power comes from your ability to harness and find benefit for these extreme emotions.

Finding Your Primary Influencers for Crocodile

Look back at the assessments that you completed in the introduction. The Crocodile Spirituality Type has four primary Influencers: Corn, Water, Eagle, and Deer. On the chart that follows, write the scores for each of the four Influencers on the line

BRYAN

Bryan is a typical Crocodile Spirituality Type. He is a counselor who loves working with offenders in a federal prison and believes his life mission is to find ways to help incarcerated men and women turn their lives around. Bryan is a great problem-solver who is an expert at discovering things about the incarcerated men and women he works with and then using this information to help them improve their situation—finding ways to turn negatives into a positive situation. He is wonderful at examining each prisoner's unique situation, understanding its complexities, and then developing a treatment plan. Bryan is highly sensitive to other people's feelings and almost has a sixth sense about what is going on in his environment. While he seems almost too gentle to be working in a prison environment, he truly loves his work and takes great pride in his ability to channel his energy into finding solutions and helping people feel better about their situation in life. Being very perceptive is a crucial quality in the transformation process as Bryan is able to bring to light prospects that people have often not even thought about in terms of reaching their full potential. He is able to heal and initiate progress where there has been none in the past. Bryan is extremely interested in helping to make society better, and he feels like he can do this by helping offenders stay out of prison when they are released. The act of bringing about transformations in himself and in others is Bryan's true spiritual calling.

next to that name. The highest score is the greatest influence in your life. You should then make note of how that Influencer is affecting your current Spirituality Type.

Corn = 8

Eagle = 4   CROCODILE   Deer = 12

Water = 10

CORN

Corn spirituality traits influence you to fight for peace and justice in your community. It pulls you to be very active in social organizations and in social leadership—becoming a leader in your community is not uncommon. You either have many children in your family or you play a parental role for your extended families or the people in your community. In general, you are down-to-earth, practical, and nurturing to other people. If Corn is Bryan's primary Influencer, he might take his knowledge about working in prison and fight for prison reform. Corn influences you to be extremely nurturing in what you do. An advocate for social justice, you are a supporter of other people because you want others to have a chance to make their lives better, and you feel it is your duty to make things better for future generations. You take great pride in your interest in, and ability for, helping people to grow psychologically, spiritually, and emotionally.

How does this interest in the community affect your spiritual road to transformation?

I always keep in mind that we are all connected and there is a a bigger picture.

WATER

Water spirituality traits influence you enjoy being challenged intellectually. You live to explore business ideas at work, test your hypotheses and those of others, and develop theories based on what you have read and how you have interpreted what you have read. In fact, you love to explore all new areas of information and play with developing theories to test that information—anything that can expand your mind's awareness and consciousness. You simply love learning about new and different things. If Water is Bryan's primary Influencer, he might develop a theory related to why offenders are unable to stay out of prison. He could combine his intellectual knowledge with his practical experience to develop his theory. Water influences you to love mental challenges, thus you tend to live in your mind a lot of the time. You are interested in hypotheses and theories about the work you do and ways that you could improve the business in which you find yourself. For you, learning never stops—you truly believe in the concept of lifelong learning, and that is what keeps you ahead of your competition.

How can your love of ideas enhance your transformation?

Ideas always keep you inspired to learn and evolve as a person. They also help keep an open mind.

EAGLE

Eagle spirituality traits influence you to love control and power. For you power and control are two sides of the same coin. The more power you can get, the more control you can get, which then makes you feel even more powerful and more in control. You are driven to make an impact on what matters most to you in life, and power allows you to do this. You are naturally attracted to other people, jobs, and recreational activities that can help you gain more power. If Eagle is Bryan's primary Influencer, he might take some classes in prison administration and attempt to work his way up the corporate ladder to ultimately become warden of the prison.

Eagle influences you to seek all of the power you can achieve even if it means jumping from job to job or doing what you need to do to move up at work. You probably feel that the best way to make an impact in the lives of people is to work hard and achieve a high ranking in an organization where you can influence the lives and careers of other people.

Why is power so vital to you?

Power = influence on others. Power also inspires change, it makes ~~your~~ ideas beome reality.

Deer

Deer spirituality traits influence you to be strong and resilient in your social advocacy and to be quite forceful and direct. Whether it is for worldly or spiritual purposes, you come on very strong with a great deal of power. You have a tendency to dominate most situations, which is why you can become a civic leader. You make a great leader because you have vision, trust in yourself, trust in your knowledge and the ability to get things done. If Deer is Bryan's primary Influencer, he might try to talk with members of the senate and congress to ask for more funding to go to state and federal prisons for educational programs for offenders. Deer influences you to use your organizational and leadership skills to help those who may not be able to help themselves. You have natural leadership qualities and other people tend to follow you and listen to what you say. Find ways to use these leadership skills on the job or in your spare time.

How can you best use this strength and resiliency to help others transform themselves?

By teaching, writing or teaching by example.

Understanding-oriented people find spirituality through words, ideas, and intellectual pursuits. If you are one of these Spirituality Types, how will you work to change the world? Think about it and write several things you would like to do to help improve the world in which we live:

- Make people aware that we are all connected spiritually.
- Humainity is important
- Trusting your intuition and developing it.
→ I will write books about these subjects. Infulence and inspiration are the only ways to see change in the world.

7

Freedom Personal Energy Pattern & Spirituality Types

There's an energy field or 'vibe' emanating from everything we encounter, from food to friends to current events. Our response to these vibes is manifested in our energy level. We each have our own energetic styles.

JUDITH ORLOFF IN *Positive Energy*

If you have the Freedom Personal Energy Pattern, you enjoy engaging in interesting activities and usually are uninhibited and upbeat. You are lighthearted, outgoing, gregarious, and love to have fun and laugh a lot. You enjoy engaging in new and different activities and adventures. You love being with other people and are at ease in groups. You are free-spirited and love to take physical and social risks.

Behaviors That Support Spiritual Experiences	Behaviors That Hinder Spiritual Experiences
• Risk taker	• Silly
• Adventurous	• Impulsive
• Energetic	• Irresponsible
• Flexible	• Unconventional
• Free-spirited	• Unpredictable
• Adaptable	• Eccentric
• Spontaneous	• Reckless
• Idea-oriented	• Scattered
• Happy	• Carefree
• Fun-loving	• Leisurely
• Charming	• Thrill-oriented

Primary Characteristics of Freedom Spirituality Types

It is through free-spirited activities that you are able to have Extended Spiritual Experiences. You tend to be relaxed and extroverted and fun to be around. You are often the life of the party, and other people enjoy being around you. You rarely ever meet a stranger, and you feel comfortable talking with almost anyone. You tend to like talking with interesting people, but keep your conversations light and loose. You require that all activities be fun, even at work. The following list describes characteristics of Freedom Spirituality Types. Check off the items that are true for you:

☐ Avoids structure, repetition, and routine

☐ Likes varied and changing work duties

☐ Observes with use of the senses

☐ Spontaneous and fun

☐ Stops to enjoy the moment

☐ Rarely gets nervous or anxious

- ☐ Dislikes predictability

- ☐ Playful with others

- ☐ Enjoys being outdoors

- ☐ Likes to meet and interact with a variety of people

- ☐ Does not like to take orders from others

- ☐ Likes to take risks

- ☐ Slow and deliberate

Occupations and Leisure Activities

Many different types of activities are well suited for people with a Freedom Personal Energy Pattern. You consider life to be a party, and you are motivated by fun and adventure. You love life and always find the time and resources to do what you want to do. The following is a list of some occupations and leisure activities that will be satisfying for you and that might lead to Extended Spiritual Experiences:

OCCUPATIONS

In the list that follows place an X in the box in front of occupations that you think might bring you Extended Spiritual Experiences:

Trades/Technical
- ☐ Carpenter

- ☐ Construction worker

- ☐ Electrician

- ☐ Machine operator

Outdoor
- ☐ Dairy farm manager

- ☐ Dog groomer

- ☐ Farm worker
- ☐ Forest nursery supervisor
- ☐ Forestry worker
- ☐ Game warden
- ☐ Greens/horticulture worker
- ☐ Landscape gardener
- ☐ Lawn service worker
- ☐ Veterinarian assistant
- ☐ Wildlife biologist
- ☐ Zoo director

Response
- ☐ Golf pro
- ☐ Recreation leader
- ☐ Pilot
- ☐ Flight attendant
- ☐ Photographer
- ☐ Journalist
- ☐ Fitness instructor
- ☐ Detective
- ☐ Entrepreneur
- ☐ Firefighter

FREE-TIME ACTIVITIES

In the list that follows place an X in the box in front of leisure activities that you think might bring you Extended Spiritual Experiences:

- ☐ Birdwatching
- ☐ Pet boarding
- ☐ Farming
- ☐ Marathon running
- ☐ Skydiving
- ☐ Beekeeping
- ☐ 4-H activities
- ☐ Fishing
- ☐ Treasure seeking
- ☐ Herb gardening
- ☐ Aerobics

Freedom Personal Energy Pattern

The Freedom Personal Energy Pattern is comprised of the following four Spirituality Types:

VULTURE	DOG
Free spirit that cannot be bound, seeks freedom, interested in many different things, seeks excitement, lifestyle is important, dislikes rules, will sacrifice anything for lifestyle, enjoys sensual pleasures, creates a festive atmosphere.	Charts unknown territories, seeks adventure, tests mental and physical abilities, lives on the edge, loves variety and challenges, risk taker, likes an element of danger in activities, lives now, life is like a game, likes opening new doors to adventure.
RABBIT	LIZARD
At home in the great outdoors, enjoys nature, feels alive in nature, practical, earthy, builder, cultivator, systematic, no-nonsense, enjoys outdoor activities, farmer and gardener, loves simplicity of nature, physical, arts and crafts-oriented, solid, competent.	Likes bringing things to life, maintains deep roots, cultivates career, hard worker, entrepreneur, growing things is creative, likes balance, enjoys recreational time with family and friends, helps others grow, long-term thinker, enjoys security.

In the next section, each Spirituality Type is described in greater detail. Make note of the strength of this Type and the Influencers for you.

Vulture Description

You are a free spirit that cannot be bound. With a natural affinity to be free to do whatever you want to do whenever you want to do it, you feel your life's mission is to be free to engage in as many activities and interests as you possibly can. Tremendously spontaneous and wanting an exciting life, you are willing to try almost anything new that could be an adventure—through adventure you feel you can stay young. Keeping your options open and not being tied down so you can do what you want if the mood strikes you is a principle that applies to your career as well as your life in general. You want a lifestyle that you direct and that you can control, and you rarely ever try to live up to the standards and expectations of other people.

CARLEIGH

Carleigh is a typical Vulture Spirituality Type—a free spirit who does what she wants when she wants to do it. She works as a recreation leader with adolescents, but she has many different types of interests. Viewing life as an adventure to be lived, Carleigh is spontaneous and does not want to be tied down to one activity, preferring to be able to freely pursue multiple activities for shorter periods of time. Others feel like Carleigh jumps around from thing to thing, but she does not worry about living up to their standards and expectations. For Carleigh, freedom comes from inside her and not from things going on in her environment. She would gladly sacrifice money and material things to pursue her dreams. Willing to try anything once, especially if it involves adventure of some sort, she lives her life based on doing what she wants whenever the mood strikes her. She does not worry about what other people say or worry about trying to live up to other's expectations of her. A spontaneous free spirit who cannot be brought down, Carleigh is very willing to sacrifice anything—money, relationships, a home—to maintain her free lifestyle. For her, the ability to be free to pick and do what she wants when she wants to do it is the most important thing in life. She thinks differently from other people and must find a job where this type of thinking is allowed. Carleigh believes that she was placed on this earth to live life to the fullest and enjoy all the excitement life has to offer. She is jovial and fun to be around, and can be the life of the party when she wants to.

Unlike most people, you see and interpret rules and regulations as merely suggestions that don't necessarily apply to you because you are such a free spirit. Rules and regulations seem to get in the way of you expressing your freedom. A lifestyle in which you are free to roam and do whatever you want to do is paramount in your life. It may even mean leaving behind many responsibilities and commitments, even if they will help you to succeed.

Regardless of what is going on around you, you know that you can always be free because you know that freedom comes from inside you and not from the environment or the expectations placed on you by others. Sometimes you feel trapped if you are not able to pursue a path of interest. In these cases, you may have to sacrifice something, often money, to pursue your dream. After all, for you the freedom to do what you want is more important than any amount of money.

Free-spiritedness also applies to displaying your thoughts and ideas. You want to be able to speak truthfully about anyone or any situation and enjoy situations where you are not only allowed, but encouraged, to be and to think differently from others. If you find yourself in a stable or conventional situation, you will always find a way to do something or say something controversial or unconventional.

With your varied interests and abilities, you prefer work that is constantly changing—you hate work that is repetitious. You prefer to focus on the big picture and rarely find yourself worrying about the small inconsequential things in life. Ultimately, you like to live large and get the most out of life. You yearn for big experiences in life, and you want a lot of everything life has to offer. Your life motto is to "eat, drink, and be merry, for tomorrow we may die."

You expect and accept all of the love, money, adventure, and good times that life has to offer, in particular, the inherent sensuous pleasures. As if your life's mission to fully indulge in the excitement provided in this life, you constantly aim high for new and exciting adventures both at work and at play. In fact, you will risk your health and safety to continue engaging in excessive pursuits.

At times you feel free to indulge in whatever types of sensual pleasures you like without consequence. Jovial and gregarious in your approach to other people and to life in general, you have a fun-loving spirituality that can be enjoyed by everyone around you. Wherever you go, you are the life of the party and are able to create a festive atmosphere. You are not afraid to laugh at jokes, even those at your expense. Having fun regardless of what you are doing is essential, as you believe that life is too short to be taken very seriously. If you find yourself in a situation that you feel is too serious, you will do your best to make fun things happen.

You are very generous and will freely share your bounty with others—you enjoy living the good life and want others to live it too. This is in line with your beliefs that you cannot take money with you when you die. You refuse to pinch pennies and do not like to be around people who are petty. Because you are so optimistic, you are able to make the most out of your life situations—it almost seems as if you are able to create your own luck. Good things generally just happen to you. Your philosophy is that life is to be lived totally and with all of the passion that can be generated.

Finding Your Primary Influencers for Vulture

Look back at the assessments that you completed in the introduction. The Vulture Spirituality Type has four primary Influencers: Rabbit, Lizard, Dog, and Wind. On the chart that follows, write the scores for each of the four Influencers on the line next to that name. The highest score is the greatest influence in your life. You should then make note of how that Influencer is affecting your current Spirituality Type.

Rabbit = _____

Dog = _____   VULTURE   Wind = _____

Lizard = _____

RABBIT

Rabbit spiritual traits influence you to use your business skills in the greening of the Earth. You can use your business and leadership skills in the great outdoors where you feel at home, rather than tied to an office and a desk. When you find yourself in the great, vast, green expanse of nature, your awareness expands, you feel alive, and you feel more spiritual than you can in the city. Thus, you are drawn to activities that involve being outdoors, whether you are engaged in working as a park ranger or enjoying outdoor activities like fishing or watching sporting events. If Rabbit is Carleigh's primary Influencer, she might take some time and go for a walk in the woods, work in her garden, or go hiking. She would probably also use the outdoors and nature in her responsibilities as a recreational leader. Whether in your business or in your hobbies, Rabbit influences you to take an interest in spending time outdoors. Because of this desire to spend time in nature, many will start businesses in which they will be working outside or helping to protect the planet. Others choose to take on activities that will help preserve nature by doing such things as recycling, cleaning up the rivers, or planting trees.

What types of outdoor things can you do to seek pleasure and enjoyment?

_____

_____

_____

LIZARD

Lizard spirituality traits influence you by pushing you to bring life and cultivate whatever is around you or available to you. You get tremendous satisfaction from making living things, people, and organizations grow and eventually prosper. How you choose to do this largely depends on your interests and the available resources in your life and community. You could choose to cultivate endeavors such as raising a child or children, tending to your garden, starting and growing your own business, leading an existing business to greater heights, or developing solutions to social problems. If Lizard is Carleigh's primary Influencer, she might pursue a hobby like rescuing abused animals or starting a spelunking club. She probably also sees her job as a recreation leader as a way of helping young men and women grow emotionally, psychologically, and spiritually. You need to become aware of the things in your life and your community that you have an interest in seeing grow and prosper.

What do you want to cultivate or bring to life?

_____

_____

_____

Dog

Dog spirituality traits influence you to seek out the excitement associated with exploring and charting unknown territories. Dog pushes you to do new and exciting things—including things that no one has done before. You want to seek adventures that will test both your mental faculties as well as your physical attributes. If Dog is Carleigh's primary Influencer, she might consider engaging in an adventure sport like caving or skydiving. It probably also propels Carleigh to use unconventional techniques in her work as a recreational director for young people. Dog influences you to try new things and challenge your sense of who you truly are—to "think outside of the box" and to move beyond your comfort zone. By pushing the boundaries, you can discover mental, physical, social, and spiritual attributes and levels of energy that you never thought you possessed.

What unknown territories would you like to explore? How can you use adventure in your spiritual journey?

_____

_____

_____

WIND

Wind spirituality traits influence you to be a natural-born leader. You are driven to be first and the best at whatever you do. With a natural urge to be in the trenches, you are most confident and self-assured when you are leading other people. Because you feel that your way is the best way and that others should follow your lead, you tend to rely solely on yourself to get things done. Very often, you have difficulty delegating tasks to others around you. You like breaking new ground and blazing new trails. If Wind is Carleigh's primary Influencer, she might take some business courses or pursue a business degree so that she can eventually become the director of the organization for which she works. Wind influences you to spend a great deal of time with the people whom you manage. If you are not currently a leader or manager, you may want to consider giving it a try. Wind propels you to try new ways of applying your business and leadership skills and abilities. It will help you think about new ways of building and maintaining your business, even if it means starting a different kind of business or doing business in a very different way.

How does blazing new trails lead to a sense of adventure for you?

_____

_____

_____

Dog Description

You need and seek out the excitement associated with exploring and charting unknown territories. Because you thrive on doing new and exciting things—including things that no one else has ever done—you seek adventurous experiences that will test both your mental faculties as well as your physical attributes. Never one to enjoy stable and predictable situations, you love to test what you are made of by engaging in and completing risky challenges. You love variety and the unexpected challenges that it brings, which results in feeling stifled in familiar jobs and recreational activities. Rather, you like jobs and activities that involve gambles and risks

TIMOTHY

Timothy is a typical Dog Spirituality Type. A marketing manager in a Fortune 500 business, he lives to explore and chart unknown territories for his organization—willing to take any risk in order to market their products and services. Timothy loves the variety that marketing allows him on a daily basis. His love of travel to other countries helps him to develop international contacts to include in marketing plans. When not at work, he loves activities that involve gambling and risks like bungee-jumping and traveling. For him, new experiences allow him to feel alive and spiritual. He lives in the moment whether he is at work or engaging in his favorite leisure activity. However, Timothy truly lives for his leisure time. He loves to be involved in any type of adventure sports. On the weekends, he often goes skydiving and caving. Always seeking new experiences where he can feel an adrenaline rush, he has also planned to begin taking flying lessons. The problem for Timothy is that he is finding that he has to engage in more adventurous activities to feel the rush he wants so badly. He says that it is hard to explain, but Timothy says that these types of activities make him feel alive and connected with nature. He lives for the moment—he thinks worrying about what is going to happen in the future or what has happened in the past are a waste of his energy. Timothy is interested in anything new and different. He enjoys reading about other cultures and their esoteric practices. He has even started engaging in some of the mysteries of life by meditating and drumming.

and the use of extraordinary mental and physical skills. You are likely to be found skydiving, rock climbing, or traveling to and exploring other cultures.

While engaging in new activities—especially those that involve an element of danger that produces an adrenaline rush—you feel most alive and most connected with humanity. You love to use all of your skills and abilities to overcome challenging obstacles. For you, risky, adventurous activities are spiritual experiences. These types of experiences allow you to call on great reserves of energy that allow you to go beyond ordinary faculties. Therefore, you will seek out the most daring activities you can find.

Physically, you enjoy a variety of adventuresome sports. Engaging in sporting events offers you a challenge to be your best and push your body and mind to their limits, but are also fun and involve social interaction. For you, all of life is like a game in that it is one grand, exciting adventure after another. You feel like if you look hard enough, you can find an adventure to embark on.

Travel is another adventure that you always enjoy because you live in the moment. You are a true world traveler and will attempt to visit as many other countries and cultures in the world as you can. At a moment's notice you can be ready to do anything or go anywhere. You enjoy living like the natives of other countries you visit and are likely to adopt the lifestyle of the culture and even attempt to speak foreign languages to better understand the people of the country. If you cannot physically visit other cultures, you will do so in your mind. You might study a foreign language, culture, or art of another country.

You also love pursuing various spiritual paths that are open to you through your adventures. Because you love to travel and do many novel things, you constantly get exposed to new and different ideals and customs. Therefore, you often find yourself interested in exploring such things as meditation, spiritual teachings from a variety of sources, and ancient rituals in your pursuit of the mysteries of life. You often feel stuck when you have no adventures to pursue.

Finding Your Primary Influencers for Dog

Look back at the assessments that you completed in the introduction. The Dog Spirituality Type has four primary Influencers: Wind, Flint, Lizard, and Vulture. On the chart that follows, write the scores for each of the four Influencers on the line next to that name. The highest score is the greatest influence in your life. You should then make note of how that Influencer is affecting your current Spirituality Type.

Wind = _____

Lizard = _____   DOG   Vulture = _____

Flint = _____

Wind

Wind spirituality traits influence you to be a natural-born leader. You are driven to be first and the best at whatever you do. With a natural urge to be in the trenches, you are most confident and self-assured when you are leading other people. Because you feel that your way is the best way—and that others should follow your lead—you tend to rely solely on yourself to get things done. Very often, you have difficulty delegating tasks to others around you. You like breaking new ground and blazing new trails. If Wind is Timothy's primary Influencer, he might think about breaking away from the business that he currently works for and start his own marketing firm. By doing so, he could build his business, hire other people that he could manage, and do things his own way. He would not have to be a follower anymore. Wind influences you to spend a great deal of time with the people you manage. Wind propels you to try new and different ways of applying your business skills. It will help you to think about new ways of building and maintaining your business, even if it means starting a different kind of business or doing business in a very different way.

What new trails would you like to blaze in your search for challenges?

_____

_____

_____

Flint

Flint spirituality traits influence you to be a leader in the community. You believe that you represent the social standards, morals, and values of society, and often feel like you are the voice for other people—especially those less fortunate than yourself. Because of your interest in uncovering conspiracies and wrongdoing about a variety of social issues, you will gladly speak out about any injustices you uncover in society. You are very committed to causes you believe in. If Flint is Timothy's primary Influencer, he might think about ways to use his talents volunteering for a nonprofit organization in his community. In this way, he could speak out for standards and values in his community. Flint will influence you to take up the cause for others who cannot defend themselves. Committed to integrity and telling the truth, you are an activist whose voice must be heard. You will gain tremendous satisfaction by being a civic leader and maybe even running for political office.

What causes would you like to fight for?

_____

_____

_____

Lizard

Lizard spirituality traits influence you by pushing you to bring life and to cultivate whatever is around you or available to you. You get tremendous satisfaction from making living things, people, and organizations grow and eventually prosper. How you choose to do this largely depends on your interests and the available resources in your life and community. You could choose to cultivate endeavors such as raising a child or children, tending to your garden, starting and growing your own business, leading an existing business to greater heights, or developing solutions to social problems. If Lizard is Timothy's primary Influencer, he might try to identify ways to help other people, especially kids, to live in the moment and enjoy adventure-based hobbies. For Timothy, growing the business for which he works, and his list of contacts, is very fulfilling. Lizard will influence you to help things and people grow and develop. You need to become aware of the things in your life and your community that you have an interest in seeing grow and prosper.

What do you want to cultivate or bring to life?

_____

_____

_____

Vulture

Vulture spirituality traits influence you to be a free spirit that cannot be bound. You feel a natural affinity to be free to do whatever you want whenever you want to do it—as if your life mission is to be free to engage in as many activities and interests as possible. You are tremendously spontaneous and are willing to try almost anything that could be a new adventure for you. You want an exciting life and through adventure you feel you can stay young. If Vulture is Timothy's primary Influencer, he might consider giving up his job and taking a new job in another country. This way, he could spend time exploring the culture and people of his new home. Vulture propels you to seek out as many new adventures as you possibly can and to seek variety in all you do. For many employees, this new adventure often leads to business opportunities in other countries. Trying to match the success you are having can be challenging.

How has being a free spirit helped in your personal and professional lives?

_____

_____

_____

Rabbit Description

You feel at home in the "great outdoors." When you find yourself in the great, vast, green expanse of nature, your awareness increases, you feel alive, and you feel more spiritual than you can in the city. Thus, you are drawn to activities that involve being outdoors, whether you are engaged in working as a park ranger or enjoying outdoor activities like fishing or watching sporting events. It is only when you are outside that you feel excited and refreshed. The simplicity of nature allows you to keep your perspective about life, work, and leisure.

You are a natural cultivator of people and things. You have a natural urge to make things grow and prosper as well as a seemingly innate knowledge about how to accomplish this growth. You are very much a farmer at heart and deep down in your soul. Regardless of the situation in which you find yourself, you always see the potential for growth. You then go about planting your seeds and nurturing them to their full potential. Much like a farmer does, you then watch over your seeds and protect them until they can flourish and grow into your vision of success.

You are primarily interested in practical, earthy matters. In fact, your earthy spirituality gives you the ability to cultivate the things you feel are most worthy, including buildings, children, relationships with significant others, or businesses. You are a builder and do so in a very systematic manner, starting with a strong foundation in any project you begin. You will then, in a very step-by-step systematic manner, build and expand upon the foundation until it has reached its full potential.

Shauna

Shauna is a typical Rabbit Spirituality Type. She is physical and loves to be outdoors, which makes her job as the intramural athletics coordinator for a small college a good fit. She spends as much time outdoors as she possibly can because that is where she has most of her spiritual moments. Shauna loves seeing people grow through leisure activities. She believes that all people have a natural connection to nature and that part of her spiritual mission is to ensure that people connect or reconnect with nature and the outdoors. Very practical and "earthy," Shauna is not interested in fame, fortune, or recognition. Shauna wants to see people grow spiritually, and she feels that the best way to accomplish this is to help others connect with nature. She is very practical and easily finds contentment in physical activities, preferably outdoors. In fact, she believes that hypotheses and theories keep people from living full and rewarding lives. Not much of a risk taker, she lives a simple life and loves being close to nature, which she accomplishes through gardening and hiking. Getting people to reconnect with nature is something Shauna does every day—teaching by example. Because she believes in eating foods that are nutritious and made of all natural ingredients, she grows her own vegetables, which she shares with others in the community. Her house is very environmentally friendly and she encourages others to do the same, often educating people about construction projects that are not eco-friendly as they do not support a site's ecology and natural systems.

You have a practical, no-nonsense approach to the activities in life. Not interested in prestige or financial rewards that come with accomplishments, you simply enjoy getting things done the way you think they should be done. You are also not interested in generating ideas or hypotheses, being innovative, or in trying to understand complex formulas. You like simple things and prefer to know how these things work.

You are a very physical person. Much of your rewards in life come through engaging in activities that provide physical satisfaction, preferably in the great outdoors. You love to use your senses in experiencing the world and what it has to offer. Finding the simple pleasures delightful, you enjoy things that are easy to experience—things that you can feel, taste, hear, and smell.

You do not like to take too many chances in the activities in which you participate. In fact, you seek stability and security in your occupational and recreational choices. Others describe you as a very solid person who is reliable and able to accomplish what you say you will accomplish. You have difficulty accepting change and will stubbornly dig in your heels to resist any type of change that is thrust upon you. You also enjoy being by yourself a lot of the time.

Finding Your Primary Influencers for Rabbit

Look back at the assessments that you completed in the introduction. The Rabbit Spirituality Type has four primary Influencers: Ancestors, Vulture, Wind, and Jaguar. On the chart that follows, write the scores for each of the four Influencers on the line next to that name. The highest score is the greatest influence in your life. You should then make note of how that Influencer is affecting your current Spirituality Type.

Ancestors = _____

Wind = _____   RABBIT   Jaguar = _____

Vulture = _____

Ancestors

Ancestors spirituality traits influence you to use your ability to dream and your imagination to visualize opportunities for yourself and others. Ancestors pushes you to imagine things that ordinary people cannot even imagine. If you believe that if you can see something then you can create it or make it possible. If Ancestors is Shauna's primary Influencer, she might consider creating a stress-management nature retreat for some of the staff at the college. At this retreat, she could talk about the effects of the outdoors in reducing work-related stress and enhancing spiritual wellness. Ancestors influences you to dream of all the possibilities that life has to offer. It forces you to use your imagination to dream up what others may think is impossible. Ancestor-influenced people will be amazed at the different types of solutions they can come up with for life's problems. Allow yourself time to meditate and "dream."

What are your dreams about the outdoors?

_____

_____

_____

Vulture

Vulture spirituality traits influence you to be a free spirit that cannot be bound. You feel a natural affinity to be free to do whatever you want whenever you want to do it—as if your life mission is to be free to engage in as many activities and interests as possible. You are tremendously spontaneous and willing to try almost anything that is new and could be an adventure for you. You want an exciting life and through adventure you feel like you can stay young. If Vulture is Shauna's primary Influencer, she might consider volunteering to do environmental studies work in another country during her vacation.

How has being a free spirit related to your love of nature?

_____

_____

_____

Wind

Wind spirituality traits influence you to be a natural-born leader. You are driven to be first and the best at whatever you do. With a natural urge to be in the trenches, you are most confident and self-assured when you are leading other people. Because you feel that your way is the best way and that others should follow your lead, you tend to rely solely on yourself to get things done. Very often, you have difficulty delegating tasks to others around you. You like breaking new ground and blazing new trails. If Wind is Shauna's primary Influencer, she might consider developing a peer-leadership model for athletes that could be duplicated in other colleges and universities across the country. Wind influences you to spend a great deal of time with the people you manage. Wind propels you to try new and different ways of applying your business skills, helping you think about new ways of building and maintaining your business—even if it means starting a different kind of business.

What new trails would you like to blaze in nature?

_____

_____

_____

Jaguar

Jaguar spirituality traits influence you to be interested in attempting to vanquish and conquer anything and everyone that challenges you and stands in your way. Jaguar drives you to battle with people as the primary motivator in your life. You get excited and begin to summon tremendous amounts of energy when you are presented with problems to solve and obstacles to overcome. You feel like you need to prove to yourself and to others that you have the ability and the power to achieve whatever you desire. If Jaguar is Shauna's primary Influencer, she might consider researching better ways to introduce athletics to new freshmen in college as a way of retaining students who might be at risk of dropping out. Jaguar influences you to keep going until you and your business have become the best they can be. To achieve what you want, you will work very hard, use great amounts of energy, and stop at nothing and step over anyone or anything that gets in your way. It is probably best that you find leisure-time activities that are not related to business so that you can effectively recharge your batteries for more business battles.

List your long- and short-range goals for nature:

_____

_____

_____

Lizard Description

You are interested in bringing to life and cultivating whatever is around you and get tremendous satisfaction from making living things, people, and organizations grow and eventually prosper. How you choose to do this largely depends on your interests and the resources available in your personal life and in your community. The various things you could choose to cultivate might include raising a child or children, tending to your garden, starting and growing your own business, leading an existing business to greater heights, or developing solutions to social problems.

You are primarily interested in developing and maintaining deep roots, and you get meaning and value in your life from watching something special spring from these deep roots. You are a hard worker and will put in the number of hours needed to ensure that growth takes place the way you would like it to. Always looking at

> ### Chamberlain
>
> Chamberlain is a typical Lizard Spirituality Type. As a financial planner who loves making people and organizations grow and increase their long-term wealth, he is a very hard worker and will put in long hours studying investments to ensure that financial growth takes place as he wants for his clients. Always thinking about long-term growth and rarely concerned about his client's financial past, he is very focused on the security of the future. He has a natural affinity for business matters and works well in analyzing investments and financial trends. Chamberlain gains a tremendous amount of satisfaction from watching people and their finances grow. Very committed to the people he helps, he is continually updating his skills so that he can provide his customers with the best advice available. A very astute person, he knows how to position himself to develop his career in a manner that will lead to great success. His systematic, organized approach to wealth building is highly prized by his supervisors. He considers himself practical and materialistic and sees nothing wrong with that. Chamberlain thrives in a business setting and is interested in seeing the business grow and prosper. Right now, it is the most important thing in his life. In turn, his career success can help cultivate his personal life. He likes to have the best things in life, including cars, homes, and electronic gadgets. For him, the secret of life is to continue to grow and not become stagnant.

the long-term growth of anything and rarely concerned about the past or present, you are firmly focused on security for the future.

You are blessed with a natural ability to cultivate your career, knowing how to make things happen that will ensure the best possible positioning for yourself on the career ladder. In addition to being shrewd when it comes to growing and developing your own skills and ensuring a secure place for yourself inside an organization, you are systematic, organized, and focused. These qualities are what make you so effective in growing and developing yourself and other people. In this respect, you tend to be somewhat practical and materialistic.

With a natural ability in the world of business affairs, you may even see a business much in the way you would a child. You would want to nurture and take care of the business and help it to grow and prosper. It would definitely be the center of your life and worthy of all your love and caring attention. This business could be a creative outlet in which you could find ways to use your skills and interests in watching and helping things grow and thrive. You are also very good at identifying and cultivating the resources of others around you.

Cultivating a satisfying personal life for you and your family and friends is also of great importance to you. You appreciate comfort at home and know it is the foundation upon which your family can grow. In your efforts to help others grow and thrive, you can be very supportive and loving. For you, the secret to life lies in effectively choosing what needs your attention. In this respect, finding a balance between work and recreation is critical.

Finding Your Primary Influencers for Lizard

Look back at the assessments that you completed in the introduction. The Lizard Spirituality Type has four primary Influencers: Vulture, Road, Flint, and Dog. On the chart that follows, write the scores for each of the four Influencers on the line next to that name. The highest score is the greatest influence in your life. You should then make note of how that Influencer is affecting your current Spirituality Type.

Vulture = _____

Flint = _____   LIZARD   Dog = _____

Road = _____

VULTURE

Vulture spirituality traits influence you to be a free spirit that cannot be bound. You feel a natural affinity to be free to do whatever you want whenever you want to do it. You feel your life mission is to be free to engage in as many activities and interests as you possibly can. You are tremendously spontaneous and willing to try almost anything that is new and could be an adventure. You want an exciting life and through adventure you feel like you can stay young. If Vulture is Chamberlain's primary Influencer, he might look for hobbies that are completely different from the work he does, such as hiking, scuba diving, or martial arts training. Another way for Chamberlain to implement the Vulture Influencer in his work would be to funnel some of his money into real estate and other monetary venues. Vulture encourages you to seek variety in all you do. For many employees, this new adventure often leads to business opportunities in other countries. Trying to match the success you are having can be challenging.

How has being a free spirit helped in your personal and professional lives?

_____

_____

_____

ROAD

Road spirituality traits influence you to use your tremendous love of people and interest in helping as many people as you possibly can. Highly attuned to the pain and suffering of people, your sensitivity fuels your mission even further, although you live a quiet life of service to others. This service often takes the form of spiritual service, but may also be accomplished through artistic vocations, counseling, teaching, and medicine. If Road is Chamberlain's primary Influencer, he might consider offering free seminars in financial planning to people in the community. Road allows you to move beyond your own achievements and your successes and think about how you can help others, encouraging you to become more empathetic to the ills of society and the people being affected—to put yourself in the shoes of others and understand what they are experiencing. Think about how you can use your abilities and empathy to help others make their lives more effective. Success seminars are often a way for you to help others in need.

How does your love of people affect you personally?

_____

_____

_____

FLINT

Flint spirituality traits influence you to be a leader in the community. You believe you represent the social standards, morals, and values of society, and often feel you are the voice for other people—especially those less fortunate than yourself. Because of your interest in uncovering conspiracies and wrongdoing about a variety of social issues, you will gladly speak out about any injustices you uncover in society. You are very committed to causes you believe in. If Flint is Chamberlain's primary Influencer, he might consider making plans with social-service agencies to offer financial planning and guidance to people in debt, on public assistance, or unemployed. Flint will influence you to take up the cause for others who cannot defend themselves—getting involved in community organizations related to social justice for people and pets is a possibility. You are an activist whose voice must be heard, and Flint will influence you to take more of a leadership role in your community. You might even consider running for political office, as you will gain tremendous satisfaction from being any type of civic leader.

In what ways do you see yourself leading others?

_____

_____

_____

Dog

Dog spirituality traits influence you to seek out the excitement associated with exploring and charting unknown territories. Dog pushes you to do new and exciting things, including things that no one has done before. You want to seek adventures that will test both your mental faculties as well as your physical attributes. If Dog is Chamberlain's primary Influencer, he might consider developing a new method (maybe a computer program) for helping people develop better financial-planning strategies. Dog will influence you to seek out novel ways of doing things, which could involve mental challenges like creating new solutions to problems or physical challenges like getting involved in adventure sports. You need to be open to trying new and different kinds of things. Dog influences you to try new things and challenge your sense of who you truly are—to "think outside of the box" and to move beyond your comfort zone. By pushing the boundaries, you can discover mental, physical, social, and spiritual attributes and levels of energy that you never thought you possessed.

What unknown territories would you like to explore?

_____

_____

_____

Freedom-oriented people find spirituality through spontaneous, out-of-the-box thinking and behavior. If you are one of these Spirituality Types, how will you be spontaneous and adventuresome? Think about it and write several things you would like to do to experience life and live life to the fullest:

_____

_____

_____

_____

_____

_____

_____

_____

_____

_____

_____

_____

_____

_____

_____

_____

Spiritual Bankruptcy

Human consciousness is rapidly transitioning to a new state, a new intensity of awareness that will be manifest as a different under-standing, a transformed realization, of time and space and self.

DANIEL PINCHBECK IN *2012: The Return of Quetzalcoatl*

All experts on Mayan culture and civilization contend that 2012 is a portal into what will be known as "The Golden Age of Spiritual Awakening." Remember that the ancient Maya kept the most complex calendar system in the known world and that they actually had seventeen different calendars running in unison. The Maya felt that in 2012 we will experience a spectral portal through which human consciousness will pass and thereby change our perception of events dramatically. During this time, the polarizing forces of greed and aggression will be exchanged for compassion and spirituality. This will usher in an age of enhanced human con-sciousness that makes us more spiritual human beings. You need to be prepared for this awakening. This book is intended to prepare you for the new spiritual awaken-ing that will occur in 2012 and beyond.

I really had not been thinking too much about the changes that would occur in 2012 until I heard two people in a café talking about all the social problems that our world currently has and where it will stop. They talked about the number of people in prison, the breakdown of the family and the high divorce rate, the destruction of the rain forests, the many animals now on the endangered-species list, and the numbers of people unemployed because their jobs had disappeared. One of the women in this conversation referred to human beings as "spiritually bankrupt"! I had never heard that term, but it intrigued me. As I listened intently to their conversation, I wondered how many other people on the planet were having the same discussion as the two people in the café. As a sociologist and a counselor, I am interested in and study the social fears of people. The idea for the book actually began as a statement and a few bullet points on a napkin:

> *Spiritual Bankruptcy and the end of the world: How have we gotten to this point and how can we fix it?*
>
> - *What are our social problems and are they as bad as they (the two women in the café) think?*
>
> - *Mayan Doomsday Prophecy*
>
> - *End of the world, or beginning of something better?*
>
> - *How can we become more spiritual and less destructive?*

These four bullet points became the framework for this book. I came to discover more about this particular topic while undergoing my own personal and professional crises. Always a bit of a wanderer and searcher, I have long tried to better understand the purpose of my presence on Earth and how I fit in. I have spent a lifetime trying to find answers to the "big" philosophical questions like "Who am I?" and "Why are any of us here?" My quest included looking at the works of the great philosophers like Socrates and Aristotle, trying different religions, and experimenting with New Age systems like the Enneagram and the Kabbala. Nowhere had I been able to find a source that would provide me with the answers.

Then one day my wife Kathy and I took a vacation to the Mayan Rivera in Mexico. I have always been interested in ancient civilizations and how they were able to build great cities, create inspirational architecture, and develop complex tools. While in Mexico, Kathy and I had the opportunity to visit many of the fantastic Mayan archeological sites. We went on guided tours of Tulum, Xacarat, and Chichen Itza. We were at these spiritual Mayan sites during the week of the summer solstice, a magical time of the year when more than seventy thousand people would make a pilgrimage to marvel at the remnants of these sophisticated cities.

While visiting many of these cities, our tour guides provided us with a lot of valuable information about the Mayan calendar, the Book of Days, and Mayan astrology. All were inextricably linked, and all of them lead me to the conclusion that the Mayan people knew a lot about time and the Earth's cycles. Their extremely sophisticated calendar system seemed to be tied to our days of birth and to spirituality. As a professor of sociology teaching a course about the theories of spirituality, this part of the Mayan culture was extremely interesting to me. I vowed to read more about the Mayan people and about their divination practices and about their astrological meanings.

Then I came across an extremely interesting work on the Mayan people and their esoteric practices. Kenneth Johnson, in his book *Jaguar Wisdom*, introduced me to more information about the Mayan calendar, the Book of Days, and the basic meanings of the Day Signs. He drew much of his information from Day Sign lore still surviving in North America, present-day Mayan myths and stories, and materials from various prophetic books of Colonial Yucatan. Johnson's approach focused on descriptive practices and lore and was "intuitive and poetic rather than a scholarly approach." Deep inside, I knew that the Mayan people and their culture and customs had some answers to life's biggest questions.

I decided to catalog some facts about humanity and see if we actually were "spiritually bankrupt" as one of the women had suggested in the café. Being a sociologist, I had access to many sociological facts and figures. Without getting into too much detail, the following is some very interesting information about our society.

Spiritually Bankrupt?

Our world is spinning out of control, and nothing seems to be slowing it down. We live in a society filled with chaos. We have too many choices, too much information, and too many gadgets at our disposal. We run around at a frenetic pace, we get impatient if we have to wait, and we experience stress during the majority of our day. Most of us feel irritable, depressed, and frustrated at work, school, and home. Finding meaning and purpose in our lives is becoming more difficult. Many people long to get back to days when life seemed more calm, controllable, and predictable. The results of this chaos can be seen in our society:

- Approximately two million men and women are currently housed in state and federal prisons, many of whom have committed senseless crimes, often killing other people for no reason. Other offenders have robbed, raped, and abused other people. Our youth, unable to find belonging and love within the current family structures, are turning to gangs to meet their needs.

- The suicide rate, especially among our youth, is increasing at an alarming rate.

- Our hospitals and mental-health centers are filled with people who have psychological problems arising from a lack of meaning in life or mental-health issues such as depression, schizophrenia, and suicidal ideation. Many of these people have little to live for and contemplate suicide on a daily basis. The numbers of people who are addicted to drugs and alcohol continue to increase with time.

- The number of people living in poverty or on public welfare continues to increase as our society continues to value material goods.

- Teachers in our school systems are underpaid, afraid of their students, and afraid for their lives while trying to teach. Students are dropping out of school at an early age without sufficient skills to get a good job and support a family.

- Wars continue to be fought around the world with the knowledge that a nuclear war will destroy most of the life on this planet.

- Terrorism continues to be a threat to our cities, banks, airlines and other transportation systems, and communities. September 11 is just one incident in which terrorism has changed the course of people's lives.

- Technology is also changing at an ever-increasing, almost alarming pace. New types of technological advancements have made communication easier, putting information at our fingertips, and enabling a truly global society. However, it is also partially responsible for the increase in depression and in the number of people who lack appropriate social skills.

- People are trying to find a way to cheat death. Cryonics, the process of being preserved at the moment of death and then being resurrected at a later date, is being perfected for people who have enough money for the process.

- The number of people suffering from workaholism is increasing. Similarly, work is no longer a stable enterprise for most people. Corporations, in an attempt to maximize profits, are displacing workers at an alarming rate.

- The traditional frameworks that have been stable for so long—the family, religion, and work—are no longer stable at all. Same sex marriages, single-parent families, and cross-generational families of today frequently replace the traditional and extended families of the past. The traditional religions are often perceived as rigid and no longer applicable to today's problems. As a result, many people look for spirituality and meaning in other sources. Finally, the 9 to 5 job working for the same company from entry to retirement has been replaced by careers that average about a dozen jobs and involve telecommuting, small and home-based businesses, and consultants who do outsourced work "as needed."

- In our families, incidences of child abuse, spouse abuse, parent abuse, elder abuse, and incest are higher now than at any other time in our history.

- According to a 2002 study by the U.S. Census Bureau, the divorce rate has just topped the 51 percent rate—there are now more people who are divorced than married. On the other hand, countries like Italy (12 percent) and Greece (18 percent) had relatively low divorce rates. In another study, *Divorce Magazine* (http://www.divorcemag.com/statistics/statsUS.shtml) estimated that while 82 percent of all married couples reach their fifth wedding anniversary, only 52 percent will celebrate fifteen years of marriage.

- Traditional religions have lost some of their appeal and influence as churches have been laden with scandals, religious leaders have been convicted of crimes and sent to prison, and the messages presented by various religions have been inadequate in addressing our spiritual needs.

As you can surmise from the information and statistics cited above, maybe we are in a state of spiritual bankruptcy! We have reached an alarming time in civilization in which our own selfishness and disharmonious behavior has created a situation that looks dire and dreadful for future generations. According to Mayan prophecy, we are actually on the verge of some major shifts and changes in consciousness. While some people see the world literally coming to an end on December 21, 2012, my research into Mayan astrology and spirituality indicates that the end that the Maya referred to in 2012 was the end of a technological and informational age and the beginning of a spiritual age. They describe a series of evolutionary cycles in which we have been passing through to get to this final cycle. We are on the threshold of a turning point in our history.

Enhanced Spiritual Experiences

Human beings must constantly struggle for the sense of universal or-
der and harmony even as they struggle towards their own evolution.

KENNETH JOHNSON IN *Jaguar Wisdom*

Mayan elders and researchers continue to tell us that something will happen on December 21, 2012. The secret to take from their prophecies is that there is a divine plan for the universe, and you and I are part of that plan. If you are reading this book, you probably want to learn what types of changes to expect. This book is intended to be your tool for better understanding the divine plan, yourself, and others. While potentially difficult to understand at a cognitive level or accept at an emotional level, hopefully you will be able to understand it at a spiritual level and have many spiritual experiences in the years to come.

We have talked about it, but spirituality is a very nebulous concept that is difficult to define. While spirituality is often equated with religion, the soul, or mystical experiences, the Mayan people looked at spirituality in terms of the identification, management, and transformation of energy. They believed that we could become the masters of our own energy by identifying our "natural talents" and then utilizing those talents for the enhancement of humankind. They believed that the most important thing was for every person born into the Mayan culture to cultivate the "lightning in their blood," or *Coyopa*, and use it to improve the Mayan society. By harnessing their Coyopa, the Mayan people were able to find the path that leads them to higher levels of meaning and purpose in life. This book is designed to help you harness the "lightning in your blood" and find the paths that take you into the new age of enlightenment.

This book utilizes ancient principles the Mayan people developed about "spiritual intelligence." Spirituality is thought to be at the core of the other dimensions of wellness along with the mental, creative, social, physical, and emotional dimensions. Spiritual intelligence is described by the Mayans as an awakening to your connection to inner spiritual dimensions, putting you in touch with your higher self, enhancing your understanding of Spirituality Types, and helping you to utilize your Personal Energy Pattern more effectively. All people come to Mayan spirituality possessing a certain degree of spiritual intelligence. The following quick assessment will help you identify your current level of spiritual intelligence, and then the remaining chapters will help you to begin increasing this intelligence. Take a moment now to complete the assessment that follows. Instructions for scoring and interpreting the assessment will follow:

Although this is a quick survey of your spiritual intelligence, it might be enlightening! If you placed a check mark in front of 0 to 3 items, you need to work on your spiritual intelligence. If you placed a check mark in front of 4 to 8 items, you have average spiritual intelligence. If you placed a check mark in front of 9 to 12 items, you are a fairly spiritually intelligent being! The remainder of this book will help you to further develop your spiritual intelligence.

Extended Spiritual Experiences

The Maya believed that purposeful living led to spiritual experiences, which then led to spiritual development—and thus spiritual wellness. After 2012, spiritual development and spiritual experiences will be at the forefront of everyone's thinking. Through the centuries, however, many psychologists have used different terms to describe these spiritual experiences, but the details described are always the same. Whether researchers have called them peak experiences, positive addictions, excep-

How Spiritually Intelligent Are You?

Place a check mark in front of the items that apply to you:

☐ I demonstrate the integration of values and beliefs with actions.

☐ I have a tremendous sense of direction, purpose, and awareness of inner guiding principles.

☐ I am able to transform energy to change old patterns of emotions, eliminate self-defeating behaviors, alter irrational thought patterns, and transcend habitual behavioral patterns that are no longer effective.

☐ I am able to accept who I am, while at the same time being flexible and integrating dormant aspects of my spirituality.

☐ I do a good job with the holistic integration of my mind, creativity, body, emotions, and spirit.

☐ I like to experience the joy of every moment by limiting what has caused separation from your own perfection.

☐ I allow myself to be who I am and I allow others to be who they are.

☐ I balance my own polarities to live a less rigid life and become more flexible, integrated, and grounded in who I am.

☐ I see the unlimited possibilities in my life and act on these possibilities.

☐ I open my consciousness to new ways of thinking and acting by understanding the unique myths and archetypes that influence my life.

☐ I see, in a very conscious way, my relation to other people and to the world in general.

☐ Most importantly, I have found ways to have more Extended Spiritual Experiences in my life.

tional human experiences, flow experiences, or simply mystical experiences, the following is a list of some of the things that have been known to take place:

- People seem to lose a sense of time and space.

- Their worries and troubles disappeared.

- Their other needs were transcended.

- They seemed to become one with an activity.

- They were totally absorbed and gave total attention to the task at hand.

- They valued the activity, not necessarily the accomplishment.

- They were cooperative with each other rather than competitive.

- The experience had a sense of delight, wonder, and awe.

- They transcended all fear, anxiety, inhibition, defense, and control.

- They were in a zone or the flow and did not have to think about what they were doing.

- The experience changes the way they view themselves.

- They felt like they were at the peak of their abilities and potentials.

- They experienced a "calm awareness."

- They were only aware of the here-and-now.

- They felt a sense of wholeness or integration.

- They felt physically and mentally relaxed.

- They were changed or inspired in some way.

The Maya believed that when a person has found work and leisure activities within the Mayan culture that were related to their Spirituality Type, they could experience a great many of these peak experiences. Although nobody experiences everything described above, psychologists have been able to draw a composite picture of such experiences in a person's life. As I began to examine these unique qualities,

I realized that I get the same type of feelings when I am writing. I came to the conclusion that everyone has these types of spiritual experiences, but the experiences vary in intensity and occurrence. Some examples include the person who loses himself while working in his garden and loses track of time, the woman who enjoys jogging and becomes so absorbed in the activity that she feels a sort of ecstasy, and the person who enjoys listening to music so much that all of his or her worries seem to melt away.

Myths about Spiritual Experiences

When I first introduced my wife to the Mayan notion that all people need to find ways to experience spiritual moments as often as possible, she was skeptical. Right away she began to doubt the veracity of people being able to induce spiritual experiences. She said that spiritual experiences just happen to people, and they have no control over when they happen. I conducted some extensive research on the notion of spirituality in the Mayan culture because it is directly related to the preparation for December 21, 2012. Again, I found that this notion of Coyopa, or the lightning in the blood, was critical in helping people enhance their spiritual intelligence. By becoming more aware of the type of energy flowing through their bodies, people began to be mindful of the activities that enhance energy or take energy away from their lives.

However, before we look at ways that you can prepare for the new age that will be ushered in on December 21, 2012, let's take a look at how the Maya felt about spiritual experiences. Many myths abound about what spiritual experiences really are, how they happen, to whom they happen, and what people can do to ensure they continue to have these experiences. The following section will explore some of the more popular myths about spiritual experiences.

Myth #1: Spiritual experiences cannot be controlled, they just happen

I wrote this book to let you in on a little secret the Maya proposed. The people who report having spiritual experiences do so for several reasons including: (1) they know what types of activities motivate them, and they engage in those activities as often as possible; (2) they are aware of how their unique Spirituality Type causes them to think, feel, and behave in certain unique ways; (3) they search both work and leisure for activities that will provide Extended Spiritual Experiences; and (4) they follow a process for ensuring that they will continue to have more spiritual experiences. Therefore, if you want to start having these types of experiences in your life, it is important to identify your primary Personal Energy Pattern, your specific Spirituality Type, and the Influencers that will help you to find balance and continue having Extended Spiritual Experiences.

MYTH #2: ONLY "SPECIAL" PEOPLE HAVE SPIRITUAL EXPERIENCES

The Maya proposed the notion that all people have access to spiritual experience. They never believed that spiritual experiences were magical moments that only a few lucky people have while the rest of their people simply lead lives devoid of magical moments. By doing the things that a person was destined to do, he or she could experience as many of these spiritual moments as they like. In addition, all people can learn to have spiritual experiences and can learn to have spiritual experiences a lot of the time. As you will see in the next section, I refer to this notion as "living" Extended Spiritual Experiences.

Some principles in this book are taught to enhance the occurrences and duration of your spiritual experiences. Identifying your Spirituality Type is probably the most important means of accessing the spiritual dimension that resides in you. Once you have identified the best way to access your spiritual side, you can begin to make effective decisions about how to use your energy. You can also enhance your spirituality by developing greater self-awareness, accessing and using your intuition, and learning to effectively harness your Coyopa.

MYTH #3: SPIRITUAL EXPERIENCES ARE OF LIMITED OR NO VALUE

Spiritual experiences function much like myths did for more ancient cultures throughout history. They contain a story consisting of intuitive or noetic knowledge that brings about attitude changes and spirituality integration. For some people, spiritual experiences also have a tremendous therapeutic value in that they can actually deter social problems such as drug abuse, alcohol addiction, and domestic violence—afflictions associated with the spiritual emptiness that currently pervades our society.

Spiritual experiences happen when pepole are operating at full capacity and when we are fully alert, aware, conscious, and alive. Spiritual experiences are a higher state of consciousness in which knowledge gained seems to be more insightful and valid than in normal states of consciousness. Therefore, spiritual experiences are a type of window through which we can reach a different state of the "here and now." Many benefits have been discovered that are associated with spiritual experiences including improved health, the reduction of stress, increased creativity, transcendence of problems, the reduction of needs, and a decrease in pain. Maslow also suggested that spiritual experiences can be ego-transcending, provide a sense of purpose, integrate spirituality, increase free will, and increase self-determination.

Spiritual experiences are unique to each person, and they can be either religious or secular in nature. To have spiritual experiences you need a framework to interpret and understand the meaning associated with the experience and a means to integrate it into your overall worldview. This book just might be the perfect tool for helping you to identify and live with more spiritual experiences in your life. The Mayan principles teach that people in our culture who have never had a spiritual experience need a method for cultivating them for personal growth, spirituality integration, and self-fulfillment.

MYTH #4: SPIRITUAL EXPERIENCES CANNOT BE INDUCED

Spiritual experiences do not happen randomly; there are a certain set of circumstances or a certain process associated with most experiences that can be described as "spiritual." This process includes the following steps that have been described throughout this book:

1. A framework for understanding the coming new age.

2. An understanding of general Personal Energy Patterns and specific Spirituality Types.

3. Focused interests in both work and leisure.

4. An understanding of the activities that lead to Extended Spiritual Experiences in our lives.

5. An understanding of the beliefs, attitudes, choices, and feelings associated with Extended Spiritual Experiences.

6. An understanding of the fears and ineffective skills that block Extended Spiritual Experiences.

7. A conscious effort to have more Extended Spiritual Experiences in our lives.

By focusing on spiritual experiences you have had or ways in which they might happen now, you will increase the probability of having more of them. You can induce spiritual experiences by focusing on and regarding them as a normal and highly necessary part of your life. This book is designed to help induce spiritual experiences and take you through the process described above.

MYTH #5: SPIRITUAL EXPERIENCES ONLY HAPPEN UNDER CERTAIN CIRCUMSTANCES

Spiritually intelligent people have powerful experiences of purpose and harmony all the time. Spiritual experiences can occur in our everyday lives and these experiences would allow us to be better adjusted and better able to function in the world. Spiritual experiences actually need to be a part of our daily lives in order for us to be healthy human beings. All people have the capacity for nonbiological experiences that have a positive effect on their spirituality and their personal identity. On the other hand, people who do not have these types of experiences often find ways to deny or repress them.

Living Extended Spiritual Experiences

Extended Spiritual Experiences are those moments when a person feels the highest levels of happiness, harmony, creativity, and possibility. They are moments in your life in which you are able to express your creative potential, realize your inherent abilities, and ultimately become self-actualized. Extended Spiritual Experiences are

DID YOU KNOW?

The Mayan sacred calendar, the Tzolkin, is a unique method of measuring time. It consists of twenty named days combined with thirteen numbers. Each day name is repeated thirteen times during the calendar cycle, for a total of 260 days (13 × 20 = 260). These twenty days were called "Day Signs."

those moments when the typical parameters of time and space disappeared, where you had a sense that limitless horizons were opening, and where you felt overcome with intense feelings of wonder, awe, and ecstasy. Extended Spiritual Experiences are those moments in your life when everything makes sense to you, all things seem okay, and you are able to see the "big picture" of life. In these Extended Spiritual Experience moments, you realize your connection to everything else in the universe, you feel at peace, and you feel an extreme sense of purpose and zest for life.

Extended Spiritual Experiences range in degree of intensity and number of occurrences from person to person. They can be found in everyday pleasures as well as in mystical experiences when consciousness is expanded, time seems to stand still, and a person feels more in tune with the world. That is what this book is about—finding out what really interests and excites you the most and is so much in your blood that you simply cannot do without it. Another aim of this book is to construct a lifestyle or "way of life" that allows more of these Extended Spiritual Experiences to be present in your daily life. Last, it is about finding a way to live your life as one Extended Spiritual Experience.

Helping you learn to slow down, be in the "flow" of life, be totally absorbed, and transcend all of your worries and fears are all part of living life as an Extended Spiritual Experience. In actuality, spiritual experiences can last from a few minutes to several hours. The Maya, though, were interested in "extending" their spiritual moments so that they were more stable and longer-lasting. When this happens, people experience a fundamental change that affects their attitudes, point of view, what they think about, and how they appreciate themselves and the world. During these intensified experiences, the elements common to spiritual experiences are constant rather than fleeting. This book can help you to learn to achieve these Extended Spiritual Experiences whenever you choose. The next chapter will describe the Mayan Spirituality System that you can use to harness the lightning in your blood to have Extended Spiritual Experiences whenever and however often you desire.

Harnessing the Lightning in Your Blood

In our transformation toward being more creative and compassionate people that live in the flow with creation, one of the central issues becomes how to spend our time—simply, what we do during our day.

JAMES ENDREDY IN *Beyond 2012*

I begin this chapter by recounting for you one of the more important Mayan legends that is passed down from generation to generation. It summarizes the Mayan beliefs about the tremendous tie between spirituality and the real world. The story of Quetzalcoatl concerns the Mayan quest for higher and more spiritual levels of living, and goes something like this:

Quetzalcoatl was one of the rulers of the Maya and Lord of the Mayan cities. It is said that he became obsessed with his own spiritual practices and ultimately began to lose contact with what was happening in the world—both within and beyond the great Mayan empire. He was not expressing his spiritual energy with the Mayan people. Then in his kingdom, strange and socially unacceptable things began to occur. Sound familiar? It should remind you of the spiritual bankruptcy we are currently experiencing. Quetzalcoatl's spiritual practice was too esoteric and did not reflect the tie between spirituality and daily life.

Then one day, evil sorcerers found their way into Chichen Itza, the greatest of the Mayan cities, and held a mirror in front of Quetzalcoatl's face. To his dismay his appearance had been transformed to such a degree that he did not even recognize himself. Are you able to recognize who you are in the mirror? *According to the tale, he even turned away from the mirror in disgust. Quetzalcoatl then began to focus on how he and his people could begin to harness their energy to make the Mayan kingdom and the Earth a more evolved and spiritual place to live.*

The moral of this story is that it is very easy to get so wrapped up in your spiritual practices that you neglect the people and things around you. The basic premise of this book is that this is happening to us today—we have become spiritually bankrupt. We care more about materialism and appearances than about living based on our spiritual core. We find that the only way to get what we think we need is to take it from other people. We are destroying the Earth and our natural resources at an alarming rate.

You are probably asking yourself how Mayan spirituality can help the people of the world become less spiritually bankrupt? The Russian mystic and developer of the Enneagram suggested that human consciousness is a process of self-organization to a more intensified state of knowing and being. The Maya also believed this to be true. They felt that with self-awareness and the development of special types of energy, you would be expressing your true psycho-spiritual nature, your Spirituality Type. The first part of this book was designed to help you identify your Spirituality Type. The rest of this chapter will focus on how energy develops in you, and then how you can harness and use the energy associated with your Spirituality Type to live spiritually and have many Extended Spiritual Experiences.

The Evolution of Energy

All of us pass through a variety of stages in our personal and career development. We also go through stages in the development of a specific type of energy. The energy you possess has evolved as you have developed into a unique human being. For many years, psychologists have been arguing about what was more important in a person's development—nature or nurture. The Maya (thousands of years before

Freud and the modern-day psychologists) always believed that people are born with certain physical, mental, and social characteristics. This heredity, however, interacts with an environmental pattern that has allowed you to flourish or has blocked your personal, career, and spiritual growth. The culmination of this match between the traits you inherit and the type of environment in which you grow will determine your Personal Energy Pattern and your Spirituality Type.

Mayan spiritual leaders, much like the traditional Kabbalistic teachers, believed that there are stages of spiritual growth and that understanding these stages would let you glimpse deeper into yourself and into the deeper intent of the ancient Mayan spirituality system. You will be able to overcome the effects of spiritual bankruptcy, realize the impact of your specific Spirituality Type, and learn how to express the energy of your Spirituality Type in work and leisure interests.

It is important to reflect back on your life to establish how your energy developed. By doing so, you will begin to align yourself with your Spirituality Type and with nature. Deep inside your spiritual core, you have a unique perspective of the world and how you fit into it. By using this perspective to identify ways to focus your energy and live more spiritually, you will be prepared for the new spiritual age in 2012.

Like all stage theories, the energy stages provide you with identifying characteristics that will make your spiritual journey much easier. However, you should be aware that these stages may or may not unfold in a linear fashion. Therefore, just getting older does not necessarily mean that higher levels of spirituality unfold. You have to work at the process. You may even straddle multiple levels, skip levels, or return to lower levels based on what is happening in your life. The four stages include:

STAGE 1

Stage 1 is the beginning of life. As an infant and child, you will start to be drawn to certain activities and play at things that will begin to reveal your primary Spirituality Type. For me, I was curious and adventuresome. My parents always tell me that as a child I would often disappear for hours, exploring whatever was available. To this day I still have an extremely curious mind and consider myself a searcher who is interested in philosophy and all different types of spiritual practices.

What do you remember about yourself that might give you hints about why you are a specific Spirituality Type?

_____

_____

_____

_____

What type of child did your parents say you were? How is this related to your primary Spirituality Type?

_____

_____

_____

_____

STAGE 2

Stage 2 occurs in adolescence and early adulthood. The various play activities related to your primary Spirituality Type are over as you begin to seriously engage in activities that you hope will bring Extended Spiritual Experiences. This is a stormy time in your life because you ache to feel unique in the world. You feel, often at a subconscious level, a need for cosmic specialness. You are never satisfied and are like a blank slate waiting for Extended Spiritual Experiences. For me, this stage occurred throughout my college years—academia was a good fit for my extremely curious nature. My mother always said that as a child she could never get me to go to school, but once I was in college, she could not get me out. I just loved to learn and was curious about many different topics. I went from bachelor's degree through a doctoral program without stopping to work very much. I knew that the love of learning was a huge part of my primary Spirituality Type (and still is today).

What happened in your adolescence and early childhood that provides you with information about your primary Spirituality Type?

_____

_____

_____

_____

STAGE 3

In Stage 3, which usually occurs in adulthood, your primary Spirituality Type begins to reveal its deeper and more profound distinctness. At this stage, you begin to become conscious, maybe for the first time, about the essence of your spiritual journey. You begin to formally access Extended Spiritual Experiences through the way you interact with people, the work you choose, and your leisure activities. You are now learning the secret that the Maya coveted for so long—you can actually induce Extended Spiritual Experiences. Currently, I am able to induce Extended Spiritual Experiences by simply writing about the Mayan Spirituality Types. When I am engaged in work and leisure activities, like writing this book, researching the Mayan culture, or visiting the ancient Mayan ruins, I am at one with the world. During these spiritual times, the concept of time actually disappears, I do not have a care in the world, I am at peace with myself, and I somehow understand how life works. For me, that is what spiritual experiences are all about!

What types of work might bring on Extended Spiritual Experiences for you?

_____

_____

_____

_____

What types of leisure activities might bring on Extended Spiritual Experiences for you?

_____

_____

_____

_____

STAGE 4

In Stage 4, mid-to-late adulthood, you are able to summon Extended Spiritual Experiences at will. You live in almost a constant state of spiritual joy and are able to transmit your unique, essential gift to other people. You begin to see the connectedness of all life and begin to see how the gifts of your Day Sign can not only bring you spiritual joy, but can bring joy to the entire world. In this stage you become one with the universe and all distinctions (like bad and good, black and white, male and female) disappear. You begin to use your gift for the greater good and begin to share your gifts with the world. In these efforts, you are able to transcend all earthly wants and needs. For me, the writing of this book has been an extended spiritual experience, and I have loved every minute of it. It allows me to share my gift for taking esoteric spiritual writings and making them meaningful to others.

What special gifts do you possess that you would like to share with the world?

_____

_____

_____

How will you share these gifts with other people?

_____

_____

_____

_____

For me, as an Understanding Spirituality Type, looking for answers to the existential questions was very easy. I have always wondered about the meaning of life, why we are here, and what my purpose is. To answer these difficult existential questions, I again went to the Mayan culture for guidance. The Maya believed that the world would be in balance and people too would be in balance, if people were able to find their purpose and live their purpose. December 21, 2012, is about exploring how you can have more Extended Spiritual Experiences in life, and then finding a way to engage in these activities. Therefore, finding spiritual purpose in your life and making meaning are at the heart of Mayan spirituality and constitute the spiritual journey.

The Lightning in the Blood

The Maya had a grasp of mathematics that was far ahead of their time, and as discussed in earlier chapters, they used sophisticated calendars to assign work to people with various Spirituality Types in the community. The ancient Maya believed that people were born with certain levels and types of energy that are tied to the basic twenty Spirituality Types. This psycho-spiritual energy would then direct your thoughts, behaviors, and actions. Ancient Mayan shamans, called Daykeepers, were keepers of the sacred calendar and would help people better understand their Spirituality Types and the patterns associated with the type. They believed that all people had a certain type of Coyopa energy that propelled them to gain spiritual experiences by engaging in certain types of activities. Coyopa, which is literally translated as "lightning in the blood," is that life force that drives you to be a certain way and to search for spiritual experiences related to your Spirituality Type.

Here's how the Maya made use of a person's Coyopa energy:

- **Service Coyopa**—Anyone who was believed to have Service Coyopa was thought to be able to evoke it through helping others in need, and they seemed to be able to show genuine love and concern for others. They were given responsibilities that required great sensitivity, empathy, and selflessness, and they performed compassionate and nurturing acts such as caring for Mayan children, nursing sick members of society, and teaching others. In our society today, these duties are equivalent to the teachers, counselors, social workers, and nurses.

- **Business Coyopa**—Anyone who was believed to have Business Coyopa was thought to be able to evoke it by demonstrating exceptional leadership and decision-making. They seemed to be extremely confident and had the ability to lead other people. They showed tremendous motivation and innovation to accomplish assigned tasks and were responsible for many entrepreneurial and competitive acts such as leading small group projects, developing trade routes, trading products with other people, and exploring new territories. Equivalent duties in today's society include managers, administrators, chief executive officers, and entrepreneurs.

- **Imaginative Coyopa**—Anyone who was believed to have Imaginative Coyopa was thought to be able to evoke it through different types of creative and imaginative activities. They seemed to demonstrate great amounts of passion, view life very artistically, and possess a flair for creativity. Their responsibilities allowed for creative expression and required sensitivity, aesthetic appreciation, and individuality such as creating pots, sewing clothes, telling stories to future generations, and writing. Equivalent positions in our society today are artists, architects, journalists, and marketing directors.

- **Understanding Coyopa**—Anyone who was believed to have Understanding Coyopa was thought to be able to evoke it through activities that required curiosity and study. They seemed to seek out information about society, the universe, and the nature of spirituality, especially prizing knowledge and learning new things that could enhance Mayan life. They were given responsibilities that required innate inquisitiveness and a drive to learn new things, question life and existence, and search for answers to the meaning of life, and included astronomy, daykeeping of Spirituality Types, and religious leaders. In our society today, these duties are equivalent to religious leaders, philosophers, historians, and astronomers.

- **Freedom Coyopa**—Anyone who was believed to have Freedom Coyopa was thought to be able to evoke it through activities that allowed for variety and adventure. With an interest in taking risks and being free to choose activities, they valued adventure, having fun, being outdoors, and being close to nature. As such, their responsibilities required them to be spontaneous in nature and possess a great deal of adaptability. Tasks included building things, farming, and taking care of animals. Today these duties are equivalent to farm workers, pet groomers, pilots, and game wardens.

These five basic Personal Energy Patterns are part of your very being, your soul, your interactions, your career choices, your business interests, and every other aspect of your material and spiritual worlds. The Maya believed that energy was so powerful that it was expressed in your emotions, your orientation to time, your beliefs, your worldview, and your personality and your Spirituality Type.

The Maya felt so strongly about the power of this psycho-spiritual energy that they felt everyone in the cultures was born with a certain purpose. Remember, they believed that you operate primarily from this one distinct energy source, but had different ways of expressing the energy (Spirituality Types), and multiple influencers on that energy source. Thus, much of their spiritual practice was an attempt to activate and integrate various types of energy. In the minds of the Mayan people, all energy needed to be explored, harnessed, and eventually transformed to enhance a person's personal and spiritual life.

The Maya believed that each living person has a spiritual purpose. Whether this purpose is to help others, be a business entrepreneur, or discover a new type of medicine, all are potential purposes on your spiritual journey. What is your gift to give? What is your purpose in life? How can you expose yourself to Extended Spiritual

DID YOU KNOW?

The Maya visualized the five Personal Energy Patterns existing in a circle. The circle is one of the fundamental spiritual symbols along with the cross and square. The circle has distinct symbolic properties including perfection, completeness, and freedom from distinction. Circular motion is without beginning, end, or variation in its perfection. Some cultures view the circle as a symbol of time or the continuous succession of moments that pass. From a more religious perspective, the circle symbolizes cosmic Heaven in relation to the Earth. Similarly, Zen Buddhism utilizes drawings of concentric circles to symbolize the stages of inner perfection and progression to enlightenment and the harmonization of the spirit.

Experiences? Your spiritual self already knows the answer to these questions, and it is now up to you to continue to discover the answers. The spiritual system that you read about in this book has probably already helped you to discover your Spirituality Type and identify the types of experiences that will be spiritual for you. Since your spirit lies within you, the more connection we have with it, the more conscious we are of our own divinity.

Connecting with Your Spiritual Energy

Spirituality is more than a belief. It's a potent conductor of energy with real-world implications.

JUDITH ORLOFF IN *Positive Energy*

The Maya, like many traditional cultures, believed that humans are inseparable from natural, cosmic cycles. After many interpretations of their sacred calendar, the Maya calculated that the Earth was approaching a cosmic cycle that would be a potential gateway to higher levels of spirituality. This could be the end of our spiritual bankruptcy and the beginning of an awareness of the fact that we are all part of the Great Spirit and that we are all divine beings. This cycle will occur on December 21, 2012, when the Earth and Sun will align to form the winter solstice. Mayan scholars believe that the values and beliefs of the world will expire and a new stage of spiritual growth will begin—the Mayan way.

The Maya believed that an evolving world is one of constant turmoil, a constant state of struggle between the life-giving powers of warmth and giving, and negative powers such as death and chaos. The Maya called this constant chaos and turmoil *Koyanisqoatsi*, which means "world out of balance." From this perspective, the world is constantly evolving and its people also need to constantly evolve. They felt

HOW WILL THINGS CHANGE?

The Mayan understanding of December 2012 suggests that:

- We will move beyond technology as we now know it. Technology will be used to enhance connections between people.

- We will have an opportunity to experience higher spiritual and human potential.

- We will move beyond a society interested primarily in money and material things.

- We will enter a new spiritual age in which finding meaning and purpose in life is the most important thing a person can accomplish during a lifetime.

- We will learn that Extended Spiritual Experiences do exist, and we will learn how to have more of these types of experiences.

- Nothing happens by accident and that there is an overall design to the unfolding of the evolutions of time.

- We are constantly making small and large decisions about how to use our energy. Choosing well will lead to Extended Spiritual Experiences.

that you and I are constantly seeking a sense of universal order and harmony as well as personal transformation. Thus, you need to become centered and reflective and not become "out of balance." You need to learn more effective ways of harnessing your Coyopa—the lightning in your blood.

So as we approach what the Maya felt would be the end of the world as we know it, you need to begin preparing yourself for the transition to a more spiritual age. To undertake this journey, you need to take what you have learned about yourself and find ways to make the information meaningful. You need to learn to harness the Coyopa in your blood and come into contact with your true spirit. The following exercises will help you remove the barriers to spiritual enlightenment and come to call on the wisdom you have, but have yet to unleash.

Signs, Signs, Everywhere Are Signs

A popular song in the 1960s called *Signs* dwells on the inescapable ubiquity of signage in contemporary society. Although this song exaggerates a bit, the truth is that there are signs all around you, but they mean little if you don't know what they mean or simply ignore them. Are you aware of the things that will bring you greater harmony, balance, and peace? The ancient Maya believed that seeing a jaguar was a sign of strength and future good luck and that seeing a child looking to the stars was a sign that the child would be a knowledge-seeker. These signs are always present, but they require you to be open to seeing what is happening in the environment that could be a signal about how to facilitate Extended Spiritual Experiences. This openness is called intuition.

The truth is that all people are open, to some extent, to receive intuitive information. Those who are more intuitive than others and can readily see the signs, while others may see the signs, but in a slightly distorted state. How receptive are you to intuitive feelings? Being extremely intuitive, I often know things before they happen. My mother always said that I had a certain "sixth sense" about things to come or the way things would work out. To this day, I still experience this sixth sense, which I talk about as having "gut feelings" and "Aha!" ideas.

During childhood this intuitive information is most available to you. Once you reach adulthood you tend to lose touch with your ability to utilize your imagination and cut yourself off from the meanings provided by your unconscious. As adults, people tend to distrust intuitive information and value sensory information, valuing data and information that is objective and conscious. The age of evolution we are currently in rewards people for repressing their intuition to the point that logic becomes a primary unconscious, automatic process. The good news is that in 2012, we will begin to experience the new age of spirituality in which intuitive information will be rewarded and will become a primary unconscious, automatic process. Therefore, intuition training continues with recognizing and processing intuitive information that is made available to you.

The Mayan system of spirituality encourages you to watch everywhere for signs. Signs are objects, situations, or events that point to something beyond itself—beyond your awareness or full understanding. At first, accepting and understanding this new type of knowledge may be difficult. However, through your intuitive powers, you can reach beyond the everyday world and begin to experience virtually limitless amounts of knowledge. Intuition allows you to tap the limitless energy of your mind and break through into dimensions you never thought existed.

Attentiveness

To be able to see the sign, you must become more self-aware of the intuitive cues, which requires that you attend to the present moment by observing what is happening. You can train yourself to be attentive to intuition, and this attentiveness—often referred to as mindfulness—both stabilizes and opens your mind to intuitive information. Through attentiveness, you can learn to access the intuitive information that allows you to go with the natural flow of your Personal Energy Pattern.

Intuition is a kind of understanding and knowing in which you are able to see clearly in the moment and know what to do to stay true to your Spirituality Type. Intuition is a natural intelligence that has the energetic ability to synchronize your mind, body, heart, and spirit.

Intuition speaks to you in a very different voice than logic. Therefore, it is important to identify the wide variety of ways that you might receive intuitive input. Some possible ways to receive intuitive input follow. I am including some of the insights that led to my career path has a writer.

Physical Knowing (Body)—This way of receiving intuition is often referred to as a "gut feeling." Examples of physical intuitive cues might include physical sensations: a stomachache or butterflies in your stomach; ringing in your ears; hair standing up on the back of your neck; a tension headache; a bad taste in your mouth; smelling smoke if something is wrong; or pain in your joints before rain. I would always get sick at my stomach before speaking in public until I realized that I hated speaking in front of large groups of people. I deduced that I did not enjoy being in the public eye and preferred more introverted activities. What sorts of messages has your body sent you about ways you might have more Extended Spiritual Experiences?

Clear Seeing (Mind)—This way of receiving intuition is often referred to as "inner vision" or clairvoyance. Examples of visual intuitive cues might include "Aha!" feelings; a light bulb being turned on in your mind; instant illumination about a topic; seeing the light; or a sudden rush of understanding. One of my supervisors at work once told me that I could reach more people by writing than by speaking to small groups. A light bulb went off in my head, and I decided to give it a try. The books I have written have sold millions of copies. What sorts of messages has your mind sent you about ways you might have more Extended Spiritual Experiences?

Clear Knowing (Emotional)—This mode of receiving intuition is often referred to as "inner sensing" or clairsentience. Examples of emotional intuitive cues might include sudden feelings about something; an instant like or dislike for someone or something; feeling like you have met someone before; feeling like you have done something before; sudden changes in mood or affect; feelings of unconditional receptivity to someone without knowing why. I feel wonderful when I am thinking creatively about my next book project or when I am writing it. What sorts of messages have your emotions sent you about ways you might have more Extended Spiritual Experiences?

_____

_____

_____

_____

_____

Clear Hearing (Auditory)—This method of receiving intuition is often referred to as "inner voice" or clairaudience. Examples of auditory intuitive cues include listening to the little voice in your head; hearing bells ringing; hearing music; hearing voices; or insightful thinking. My mother always kept telling me that she had read every book in her hometown library, that she always felt she could write a book, and that I am just like her. I have heard her voice saying that for the past twenty years. What sorts of messages has your hearing sent you about ways you might have more Extended Spiritual Experiences?

_____

_____

_____

_____

Spiritual Knowing (Soul)—This avenue of receiving intuition is often referred to as listening to your "inspirational voice." Examples of spiritual intuitive cues might include mystical experiences; a sudden understanding of yourself and others; a feeling of creativity when facing a problem; a feeling of connection with someone or something greater than you; or a sense of true purpose in life. When I am writing, I feel at one with all people and the world. For me, writing is a truly transcendent experience. I would do it even if I did not receive a penny from my writing. What sorts of messages has your soul sent you about ways you might have more Extended Spiritual Experiences?

_____

_____

_____

_____

_____

By developing your intuition, you will open a connection between your daily self and your spiritual self. Unfortunately, most people do not take the time to make this connection and merely live through their daily self. The ancient Maya believed it was imperative that people develop their spiritual selves to the fullest. For some of you reading this book, you will have identified your Spirituality Type and begin to induce more Extended Spiritual Experiences in your life. For you, the journey has begun and you are well on your way! For others, you need to continue working on the exercises in this chapter to further connect with your Spirituality Type. If you continue to be receptive to your spirit, you will receive insights and be guided to wonderful experiences for reasons that you cannot explain.

Staying in the Present

Staying in the present moment is critical to connect with your spirituality. Only by staying in the present can you remove your armor, shield yourself from your past, and realize that you have all that you need right here and now. The best way to stay in the present is through mindfulness. Mindfulness is that state of mind in which you are fully present and not thinking about other issues in your life. It is being in touch with the present moment so that you can see its fullness, hold it in your awareness, and come to know and understand it fully. It is being present to what you are doing at the time you are doing it in a nonjudgmental way. Some might call it "being in the flow." The type of attention associated with mindfulness increases your awareness and allows you to accept the reality of the present moment. When you lose awareness of the present moment, you create problems for yourself because you are forced to rely on unconscious and automatic thoughts and behaviors that have developed over the years.

Mindfulness is more difficult than it sounds. Many forces work against our being mindful during any activity. Some of these forces are the creation of our own minds and include labels we attach to our performance, rehearsing what we might say next rather than listening, and judging ourselves. Remind yourself that this present moment is all there is. What is happening now is simply happening. When asked "Are you aware?" or "Where is your mind right now?" you will observe that your mind has a habit of trying to escape from the present moment. However, mindfulness is the state of mind in which you are fully present with the person or the activity in which you are engaged.

EXPERIENTIAL EXERCISE—BEING MINDFUL

Stop for a moment. Sit down and become aware of your breathing. It doesn't matter for how long. Let go and fully accept the present moment. For several minutes, don't try to change anything, just let go and breathe. Breathe and be still. Give yourself permission to allow these moments to be as they are. If that does not work, focus your attention on any object for several minutes. Pick out an object and stare at it for several minutes. You may also focus on the question "What is my purpose?"

Did You Know?

In Buddhist psychology, much like the awareness promoted by the Maya, mindfulness is said to have three primary benefits:

- Inhibits unhealthy mental qualities like greed and anger.
- Cultivates and strengthens healthy qualities like joy and love.
- Promotes wellness and the balance of healthy qualities.

Now answer the following questions related to the mindfulness exercise you just completed.

What did you find your mind thinking about?

_____

_____

_____

_____

What thoughts kept coming back into your head?

_____

_____

_____

_____

How did your mind attempt to escape the mindfulness of the present moment?

_____

_____

_____

_____

One reason your mind attempts to escape the present moment is the fear of being mindful. Your mind would prefer you to be thinking about the past, which you cannot control, and the future, which has not yet, and may never, come. Don't get caught up at this point in having a special experience or in making some sort of progress. You will slowly notice differences in your awareness over time.

Emptying the Mind through Meditation

By shutting down the outer noise of the harried world—traffic, televisions, cell phones, iPods, radios, conversations—we are left with the inner chatter of your own mind. This constant chatter of your inner voice and other voices keeps you from connecting with your spirituality. This chatter keeps reminding you of what you need to do, could do better, forgot to do, regret not doing, and what was done to you in your childhood. The interesting thing is even though you know that these inner voices are annoying you, turning them off can be very difficult. Oftentimes you probably find yourself turning on or letting in outside noises to help drown out the voices.

The best way to turn off the voices is through meditation. This book is not intended to teach you to become an expert in meditation, just to introduce you to a method of connecting with your spirit and overcoming spiritual bankruptcy. Meditation is the practice of attempting to focus your attention on one thing at a time to quiet your mind, which in turn quiets your body. In meditation, focusing on one thing allows your mind to stay focused and exclude all other thoughts. There are many different forms of meditation. In meditation you can focus by repeating a word like "OM"; count your breaths by saying "one," "two," "three" after you exhale with each breath; or gaze at an object like a candle or a piece of wood without thinking about it in words. You may also want to try focusing on nothing but the question, "What is my purpose?"

Here is an example of a typical Mayan meditation:

Sit in a quiet place where you can relax. Allow your breathing to become increasingly slower and easier. Release any stress that you feel in your body. Bring your attention to your throat, tongue, and the back of your mouth. Release any tension you feel. Let your body relax and let your emotions become more tranquil. You should begin to get a clear and strong sense of who you are as you go inside yourself. Release tension and feel the energy surging throughout your body. Focus on your inner awareness. As other thoughts enter your head, make note of them and then continue to concentrate on who you are. Experience the flow of energy starting at the top of your head and moving through your body down to your feet. Be aware of your immediate experience. See the energy spiraling toward your brain and releasing, bursting onto your brain to produce a form of self-illumination or enlightenment. The resulting mental and spiritual state will now be prepared to answer such questions as "Who am I?" and "What is my purpose?" Allow yourself to accept the knowledge imparted to you.

Breathe!

Sounds easy, doesn't it? Not so fast. The Maya believed that the breath is intimately connected to your spirit, Coyopa, and life force. Paying attention to your breathing is by far the world's most common meditative exercise and a central element in yoga and tai chi. You should not attempt to change it—just become more aware of it. This will allow you to easily be brought into conscious awareness. Make note of the parts of your body or ways your mind is attempting to interfere with the natural movement of your breathing. If your attention wanders and takes you away from the focus on your breathing, simply bring back your attention so that you return to your focus.

The "breathing countdown" technique combines elements of meditation and can also be very effective. It is a simple and effective way to help you connect with your inner spirit. The technique is as follows:

1. Close your eyes while sitting or lying down.

2. Take a deep breath, hunching your shoulders and holding this breath for several seconds.

3. Slowly and completely breathe out, letting your shoulders and arms become limp.

4. Resume normal breathing.

5. On your first breath out, silently count "ten." On the next breath out, silently count "nine." On the next breath out, silently count "eight," and so on down to "one."

6. When you reach "one," you can repeat "one" and begin counting back to "ten."

7. Continue this exercise for three to five minutes.

8. When you are finished, slowly open your eyes and ask yourself, "What is my purpose?" Write down the responses that come into your head.

Although there are many ways of becoming more aware, this simple technique still remains one of the best ways to slow down and connect, or reconnect, to your spiritual nature.

Think about Your Thinking

Believe it or not, your thinking has a distinct effect on how you feel and what you do. Cognitive scientists have studied the effects of cognitions and have concluded that what you think creates the experiences you have. How you react emotionally often depends on your thinking. For example, anger is often a result of your expectations—in any given situation, if they are not met, then you behave in a way related to your feelings (angry). Therefore, you should examine your thought patterns to understand what types of things trigger your feelings and behaviors. These thought patterns, often referred to as self-talk, are like having conversations in your head. Remember, by identifying the cognitive triggers that lead to unwanted feelings and behaviors, you can eliminate them.

Simple Pleasures

Simple pleasures offer you quiet stability and harmony in a hectic, ever-changing world. Simple pleasures, those activities you do for fun and relaxation, can help you connect with your spiritual self. Some simple pleasures that tend to spark Extended Spiritual Experiences for me include sitting on our back porch and looking at the mountains, my dog lying at my feet as a write pages for a new book, a long conversation with my wife about how our days went, taking my dog for a long walk in a park near our house, long-distance phone calls with my eighty-four-year-old father, reading the works of early philosophers, traveling to Mexico to study Mayan astrology and spirituality, and hanging out in bookstores. What simple pleasures do you enjoy that could evoke Extended Spiritual Experiences?

Energy Work

The Maya believed that just as the Tree of Life is a pivotal point in the universe, likewise there is a central axis that forms a pivotal point in human beings as spiritual entities. Just as the vital energy from within the Earth travels through the Tree of Life, a similar energy flows in the spinal column that breathes life into you. The last time I was in Belize, I talked with a person who was a modern-day "Daykeeper" or "keeper of the sacred calendar." He showed me the following exercise designed to open up the flow of energy throughout your body:

> Get into a comfortable position, either sitting or lying down. Close your eyes and begin to relax. Breathe slowly and deeply for a few seconds. Imagine that a vital energy force, called "malinalli" in Mayan, flows up and down your spine toward the heavens and from the underworld. The flow of malinalli concentrates in three specific centers in your body. These centers are analogous to the chakras of the Hindu tradition. These Mayan centers are located at the crown of the head, the heart, and the base of the spine.

Take a moment and locate these energy sources in your body. Feel the energy emanating from these three sources. During your next breath, imagine that you are gathering malinalli and pulling it into your body from the ground through your feet. Pull this malinalli up to the center located at the base of your spine, and let it expand there. Feel it pulsating with energy and clearing out any potential blockages. Do this for about forty-five seconds while continuing to breathe slowly. Now pull the malinalli up to your heart. Let it expand and also feel it pulsating and clearing out any blockages. Do this for about forty-five seconds and continue to breathe in positive energy and breathe out negative energy. Lift the malinalli higher in your body. Feel it flowing to the crown of your head. Let it expand there and clear out any blockages you may have. Continue to breathe. Take a few minutes now to enjoy the feeling of your energy centers being totally open and enjoy the vitality of the flow of malinalli throughout your body. After a few minutes, let the malinalli flow back down your body through your heart, your spine, and back down to your feet and into the ground. Then open your eyes and stretch your muscles to feel how energized your body now feels.

I have found that if I complete this several times a week, I get better at raising energy and visualizing it coming from the earth. I also use this exercise to enhance my ability to place the energy into areas of my body that need "work."

Another way of working with energy is to try to enhance the amount of energy you possess. You have heard other people say things like "he is an energetic speaker" or "that book energized me." The Maya believed that the best way to become energized is to connect with your Personal Energy Pattern and your Spirituality Type. However, the exercises included in this chapter are designed to both help you connect with your spiritual self and to learn more effective practical ways of living once you have discovered, accepted, and integrated your Spirituality Type into your daily life.

Concluding Thoughts

Maya elders believe the world will not end in December 2012, it will be transformed, as a channel from far above opens and cleansing cosmic energy flows toward the Earth, raising all to a higher level of vibration.

SHIRLEY ANDREWS IN *Lemura and Atlantis*

The Maya believed that human beings have passed through four evolutions and December 21, 2012, will usher in the fifth and final evolution. They felt that the parts of the old evolution that did not work will be destroyed and the rest will become the seeds for this new age. This is a time of purification—not the end of the world—and a time for spiritual transformation. Therefore, December 2012 should not be a time to be feared, but rather a time to eliminate your old habits that are not working and concentrate on those that do work and provide you with energy and vitality. You can outgrow your ingrained habits and belief systems to live a much happier, more fulfilling life.

One reason that the Mayan Prophecy has become so popular is the fact that the Mayan people were legendary timekeepers and astronomers. These ancient people were so sophisticated that they developed a calendar that was more accurate than our own is today. By observing the planets and stars, they were able to document and assign meaning to a variety of astronomical phenomena and provide a system that can be used to help people live more spiritual lives.

I honestly believe that we are on the verge of a new age of consciousness beginning December 21, 2012. The world is evolving into a new cosmic age, and all human beings must do the same. Right now, we are living in an age of spiritual bankruptcy that just seems to keep spinning out of control. The Mayan prophecies and the teachings about Mayan spirituality can hold the key as we prepare for a new cosmic age. We now need to use that key to open the door to greater levels of consciousness and spirituality. As the new age unfolds, you will be reunited with the wisdom of the Maya—and return to living with the natural cycles and energies represented by the calendar. Using insights from this book, you will be able to elevate your own personal consciousness, as well as world consciousness, through the evolution of the Personal Energy Pattern that is centered in your body and your spirit.

The Mayan Tree of Life and the Spirituality Types that flow from the Tree allow us to harness the awareness, vitality, and empowerment we need to live happy lives. It provides the insights we need to come to grips with, and use, our talents and gifts to have as many Extended Spiritual Experiences as humanly possible. The Mayan Tree of Life and Mayan Spirituality Types provide a fun and challenging way for people to explore who they are, as well as providing a system for spiritual growth and development.

The Mayan "recipe for spiritual enlightenment" seemed to work for their ancient culture, and I believe that it can work for you in our modern culture. The Maya have taught us about the importance of identifying and living according to your Spirituality Type, the need to learn about and harness the energy source that moves through your body and have as many Extended Spiritual Experiences as possible. You simply need to begin the process by connecting with your energy and your Spirituality Type. This will put you on the path to balance and serenity. Having Extended Spiritual Experiences allow you to slow down time, be in the "flow" of your life and the lives of others, be totally absorbed in what you are doing, and transcend all of your worries and fears.

In this book, I have attempted to demystify the Mayan system of spirituality and astrology and make it a practical tool that you can use for self-discovery, increased happiness, and greater life satisfaction. In addition, it is an excellent spiritual tool for learning to increase the number and length of your spiritual experience. In this book, I have tried to provide a very nonthreatening way to understand the complex nature of the Mayan Tree of Life and the Personal Energy Patterns and Spirituality Types associated with this ancient astrological system. To live satisfying, fulfilled lives, all people must understand and accept our own and other people's basic Spirituality Types. It is my hope that this book has made the study of Spirituality Types enjoyable and fun!

GOOD LUCK ON YOUR JOURNEY . . . THIS IS THE BEGINNING!